MATH POETRY

Linking Language and Math in a Fresh Way

Betsy Franco

One elephant has four legs
If you have three other elephants
Sixteen legs would make . . .

A STAMPEDE!

A GOOD YEAR BOOK™

Good Year Books

Are available for most basic curriculum subjects plus many enrichment areas. For more Good Year Books, contact your local bookseller or educational dealer. For a complete catalog with information about other Good Year Books, please contact:

Good Year Books
P.O. Box 91858
Tucson, AZ 85752-1858
www.goodyearbooks.com

Cover design: Sean O'Neill
Interior design: Dan Miedaner
Back cover student drawings: Ilse Nuñez, Minji Choi, and Jane Suk

ISBN-10 1-59647-072-0
ISBN-13 978-1-59647-072-9

1 2 3 4 5 6 7 8 9 - MG - 09 08 07 06

Library of congress Cataloging-in-Publication Data

Franco, Betsy
   Math poetry : linking language and math in a fresh way / Betsy Franco.
      p. cm.
   Includes bibliographical references.
   ISBN-13: 978-1-59647-072-9 (alk. paper)
   ISBN-10: 1-59647-072-0 (alk. paper)
     1. Mathematics--Study and teaching (Elementary) 2. Poetry in mathematics education.
3. Mathematics--Juvenile poetry. 4. Children's
poetry, America. I. Title

QA135.6.F728 2006
372.7--dc22
                                   2006041115

Dedication

For Bob Grumman who woke me up to math poetry with his beautiful "long division poetry" and "mathmakus."

Acknowledgments

Thank you to all the creative children at El Carmelo Elementary School who wrote the poems throughout the book. I am also very grateful to their teachers who let me try out the Poetry Frames in their classrooms and gave me excellent suggestions:

Alice Anne Chandler, *grade 3*
Annette Isaacson, *ELL*
Gaelyn Mason, *grade 5*
Sarah Newman, *grade 2*
Janeen Swan, *grade 4*

Thank you to the children at Barron Park Elementary School who did such a beautiful job writing and illustrating math poems based on a theme—and to their teachers, Larry Wong, Shari, McDaniel, and Patrick Lewis.

Ryan Peterson at JLS Middle School gave me the idea to write mathematickles about algebra. I am most grateful to him for this wonderful idea.

Preface

A̲t a very early age, children start to identify with either a verbal or logical way of thinking. They say, "I'm not good at math, but I like to write," or "I hate to write, but I love math." Fortunately, when children write math poetry, they invariably surprise themselves. They find parts of themselves they didn't realize existed. Every time it happens, it's a thrilling phenomenon to watch.

Now it's time for you and your students to embark on your own adventure—writing creative math poetry that will enliven your classroom and engage your students on multiple levels.

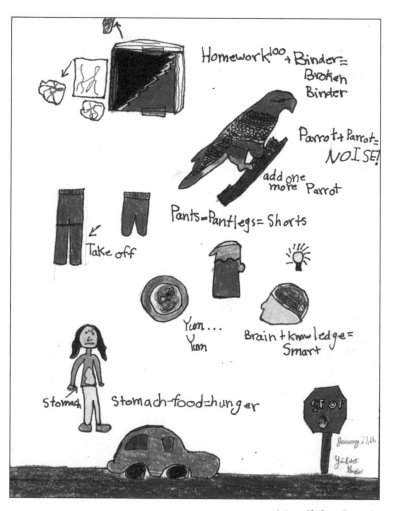

Yamileht Garcia

Contents

Contents

Ilse Nuñez

Introduction

Before it was common practice, my seventh-grade algebra teacher made a link between literature and math. After he introduced us to the math in Lewis Carroll's *Alice Through the Looking Glass*, I never looked back. In fact, I have been writing and publishing my own math poetry for decades. Because I wanted to share what I was discovering, I began introducing math poetry through workshops at elementary schools. In each classroom, mathematicians became poets, and poets became mathematicians. All children—mainstream, ELL, and verbally challenged—were able to participate. Teachers wrote their own poems and enriched the ideas I presented. A new writing form emerged that left us all invigorated.

By writing math poems, children discover aspects of math they've never imagined before. Working with math in a fresh way, they deepen their understanding of the operations and important math concepts. Particularly, they become more comfortable and adept with word problems, for they are essentially writing their own word problems. Importantly, writing math poetry shows children that math can be beautiful, funny, poetic, sassy, and creative. It also highlights important connections between math and other curriculum areas—science, social studies, and language arts—and connects math to students' lives.

This book is filled with Poetry Frames and ideas for helping children write their own math poems. Through these frames, math will come alive for your students, and poetry will gain a new dimension. The poetry is stunning, as you will see from both the samples and from your students' poems.

One of the most important aspects of math poetry is that there are no wrong answers. This open approach can help many children relax around math and around poetry. The children can break the rules, they can dive into their imaginations, they can explore numbers in a poetic way. As children and teachers use both sides of their brains at the same time, mathematics and poetry combine, resulting in a "chemical reaction" that opens children's minds in ways they haven't experienced before and we haven't seen before.

How the Book Is Organized

This book is divided into two sections. Section I shows how to write "traditional" math poems. Section II describes how to teach what I call "mathematickles," a fun and innovative type of math haiku.

Section I introduces frames for writing traditional math poems such as Ben's poem about jellyfish shown below. This is a *diamanté* poem that has been adapted to include mathematics.

100 jellyfish
upside down, lighting, drifting
50 are electric, 50 are flower-hatted
calm, happy, mysterious
100 stingers

Ben, grade 3

This section introduces a variety of Poetry Frames, each focusing on a particular math concept. For example, children write poetic subtraction word problems, blues poems about money, free verse poems about estimating baby animals, division odes, and much more. You will immediately see how math has been interwoven into the poetry in a meaningful way.

In Section II, the chapters move on to a form of poetry called "mathematickles" in which words are substituted for numbers in math problems. These poems are very close to "math haiku." They are based on a children's picture book I wrote entitled *Mathematickles!* (Margaret K. McElderry Books, 2003) in which I explored the operations and many other math concepts.

Below are some poems similar to those in *Mathematickles!* This guide, *Math Poetry*, works perfectly without the picture book, but the book can be used as inspiration and to reinforce the learning.

$$\begin{array}{r} \textbf{sprouting bulbs} \\ \textbf{flight of wings} \\ + \quad \textbf{warm rain} \\ \hline \textbf{signs of spring} \end{array}$$

$$\begin{array}{r} \textbf{birdhouse} \\ - \quad \textbf{birds} \\ \hline \textbf{seedsdroppingshusks} \end{array}$$

$$\textbf{rows} \overline{)\begin{array}{l} \textbf{veggies} \\ \textbf{garden} \\ - \textbf{produce} \\ \hline \textbf{weeds} \end{array}}$$

woodpecker x rotten stump = birdworld rap

lake ÷ storm = ripples

fun x (mountains + ocean) = hiking + swimming

Debbie Graham, an elementary school teacher who saw the mathematickles children had written, said, "It's so simple, it's profound. By providing a simple structure and then allowing children to write about what's in their heads and their hearts, they gain confidence, and anything can be built from that. Learning in poetry and math is about making connections, and that's what this (writing mathematickles) allows for."

Mathematickles are appropriate for mainstream, ELL, and gifted students. They can be an eye-opener for students who think they don't "get" math or don't like math. Thinking about math operations and concepts in words, rather than numbers, can turn on the light for students and help them think mathematically.

I've included a thorough explanation of how your students can use each Poetry Frame (template) to write their own math poems. For this purpose, every chapter in the book includes Sample Poems and a Poetry Frame, formatted as blacklines, to distribute to the students. The section entitled My Classroom Journal consists of a description of my experiences in the classroom to show how the lesson looked on a practical level and how students reacted. Sample poems written by children are interwoven throughout this portion and can be used as additional models. The Teacher Notes give step-by-step, explicit directions for teaching the Poetry Frame, including brainstorming exercises. In addition, I've included ways to adjust the difficulty of the lesson to make it easier or more challenging.

After Sections I and II, you will find a bibliography of math poetry books that can be used as poetry prompts and springboards for further math poetry writing.

How to Use the Book

You are embarking on an intercurricular adventure that will yield wonderful results. Because math poetry is a new "genre," I would suggest flipping through Sections I and II and getting the feel for math poetry. Once you've read through a chapter or two, you will see that you have the tools you need. I was a teacher myself, so I made your job easy.

The chapters of *Math Poetry* are arranged in a logical order mathematically; however, the book can be used in any order that suits your needs. You can pick and choose chapters according to the concepts you're studying in math. Or, if you're writing poetry with your students, you can interweave math poetry into your writing curriculum. You'll find that your time is well spent because the poems will build both math and language arts skills. In addition, science and social studies play a role in the Poetry Frames. For example, there are poems about predators and prey, about animals that come in groups of one hundred, and about animals who have thousands of babies. There are poems about the "fractions of me," buying items at a store, and more. Throughout the book, the poetry prompts can be used to introduce, reinforce, and/or give a context to math concepts—to bring them to life, to personalize them, and to solidify them in children's minds and hearts.

After choosing a chapter, read through the Sample Poem(s) and look at the Poetry Frame to see where the chapter is headed. Before the lesson, photocopy the Poetry Frame and possibly the Sample Poem(s). Or show the Sample Poem(s) on a transparency, a white board, or chart paper. Then read the Classroom Journal and the Teacher Notes to understand the lesson. Using the Teacher Notes, present the poetry prompt to the class. Add your own ideas to make it even richer.

Once the students are writing, circulate as you normally do to help children get started and to respond to the parts of their poems you delight in—the math, their knowledge of the math, the words, the use of language, the poetry, the ideas, the sense of humor, the cleverness, the personality that shines through. Note that students may want to work together on mathematickles, particularly for multiplication and division.

To validate the children's poetry, make a book from the poems, either as individual books for each student or as a class book. You can also display poems in the classroom. Or you can have a poetry reading in the classroom. This can consist of informal sharing, or it can be a more organized reading, where poets are introduced. Above all, loosen your mind along with the children, and then hold onto your seat. You're in for a fun, mind-opening, cross-curricular learning experience.

Math Poetry and the Standards

Because the Standards are an integral part of today's classroom, I included math and poetry concepts that are enumerated in the standards. Your time writing math poetry with your students will be well spent.

The math concepts covered are:

Children will also learn many aspects of poetry writing and writing in general:

Math Poetry for All Students

Because math and poetry are universal languages, everyone in the class can participate successfully, regardless of their life experience, skill level, or language fluency.

One of the most inspiring moments of my poetry workshops came when Alexander, a third grader, showed me his poem about a mother turtle and her babies. It was so heartfelt that I assumed he was one of the enthusiastic writers in the class. He cleared that up quickly by explaining that he never liked to write, but he didn't mind writing the poem about the turtles. He was very proud of that poem, and his teacher said it was a defining moment for him in his attitude toward writing, which had not come easily to him before this. See Alexander's poem entitled "Baby Turtles" on page 46.

I found that ELL students were very enthusiastic about math poetry and wrote some charming poems. You can see it in Omar's addition poem. He wasn't sure about how to complete the last verse. When I asked him what *he* was doing as all these skunks were playing together, he said, "I'm hiding in the ground," and we laughed.

> My topic is skunks.
> My numbers are 87 + 64 = 141

141 Skunks
87 skunks are in the dens.
64 skunks are under the ground.
One goes away
and then there's 140.

They play tag together
with their friends.

I am in the ground
hiding.   *Omar, grade 2*

You can feel Maria's involvement in her subtraction poem. Maria is an ELL student from Russia:

7 little black flies
were buzzing near a tree.

Along jumps a big fat
hungry frog.

2 little black flies hurry away.

How many were left? <u>5 little black flies</u>   *Maria, grade 2*

When we wrote blues poems about losing a twenty-dollar bill, Steven, an ELL student in third grade, had a very funny description of the face of the bill. It made us all laugh. He also used rich adjectives to describe the skateboard he could have bought. His poem is excerpted below:

> **. . . With a big-headed dude on the front**
> **of that crazy $20 bill . . .**
>
> **Oh, why did I lose my $20 bill?**
> **Oh, what I could have bought with my $20 bill.**
> **1 cool skateboard**
> **that had shiny gold wheels for $10.**
> **I would of had a $10 bill left.**

Gloria, a second-grade ELL student, wrote one of the only rhyming poems and it worked! I usually discourage rhyming because it can sound very forced, but Gloria was a natural.

> My topic is Ducky.
> My numbers are 100 + 99

> **199 Duckies**
> **199 little duckies**
> **went out one day**
> **over the hills and far away.**
> **Then mother duck**
> **said quack quack quack**
> **and all of the 199 came back.**
>
> **Together they**
> **all made a big river**
> **and All Got In!**
>
> **I swam with them splash**
> **and they splashed**
> **Me In!**
>
> *Gloria, grade 2*

I was very pleased to discover that ELL students were able to write some beautiful "mathematickles." I attribute this to the simplicity of the form and the fact that they can bring in elements of their cultural backgrounds. As an added feature, writing mathematickles is also an excellent vocabulary builder for ELL students.

Claudia's mathematickle is like a beautiful math haiku:

> **clouds + mountain = rain**   *Claudia, grade 5*

Ji-Min's is funny:

10 mice + 2 cats = 2 fat cats   *Ji-Min, grade 4*

Teachers who saw the mathematickles written by ELL students concluded that we usually ask them to write about what they don't know instead of letting them tell us what they do know. Ironically, rather than letting them explore their imaginations, we ask them to stick to the point—learning English. Annette Isaacson remarked, "You can see how smart they are from their mathematickles."

Annette also said that many ELL students were at the top of their class in their native country. She said when she translates their poetry from their original languages, she finds that they often write in metaphors. She was pleased to see these skills come to the forefront when students write mathematickles in English. Because grammar is not the main focus, students can shine again.

A Discussion about Writing "Word Problem Poems"

Word problems are the building blocks for understanding math in context. Children are accustomed to reading and solving word problems, but writing their own gives them a fresh perspective. It deepens their understanding of the components of a word problem, makes them more aware of which operation is involved, and helps them identify the necessary data to solve the problem. Writing their own problems demystifies word problems in a useful, fun, and motivational way.

By writing these poems, they are deconstructing word problems. They are starting from the inside and moving out to see how the problems were written. This can't help but give them insight into the structure and meaning of a word problem.

In many of the frames in this book, children will be virtually writing their own original word problems. In some of the Poetry Frames such as addition and subtraction poems (pp. 29 and 36), children start by writing a simple problem and then embellish it with rich language. This type of exercise will engage them in the "story" of their word problems. It combines math and writing in a powerful way to make word problems finally come alive for children.

A Discussion of Poetry Writing and Writing in General

Math Poetry introduces important math concepts, but it also introduces the basics of poetry writing and of writing in general.

Writing in General

The children will be practicing many useful writing skills in the book. They will be brainstorming ideas prior to writing, using reference materials, and revising their work. Throughout, they will engage in descriptive and narrative writing, and they will be aware of point of view. Revision will come into play once they have a first draft to work with. When the time comes to share their work, they will have an opportunity to practice fluency.

The Basics of Poetry Writing

Below, you will find many student samples of different elements of poetry. These samples are often excerpts from the poems. The math may not be evident until you read the entire poem in a later chapter.

Poetry Forms

The students write a wide variety of poetry forms in this book:

- The Poetry Frame entitled "Number Sense Poems" (p. 18) introduces the *diamanté* poem, a poem in the shape of a diamond. I adjusted the traditional format of this five-line poem. In the new form, the third line relates to numbers.

- The chapter on writing shape riddles (p. 23) gives children experience in writing traditional *riddles*. First students write a simple riddle. Then, by embellishing it with intriguing detail and making careful word choices, they make their riddles poetic and compelling.

- In the students' money poems (p. 49), they are "singing the money blues" because they lost a twenty-dollar bill. The Poetry Frame introduces children to the elements of the *blues poem*, which the African-American poet Langston Hughes helped develop. The chapter stresses the elements of the blues poem: the repetition and the sad, yet subtly resilient, spirit of the poem.

- The measurement poems (p. 56) are very close to *persona poems* in which the poet pretends she is someone other than herself. In this case, the children are pretending to be only 10 centimeters tall.

- The *ode* is a poem in praise of someone or something. In their division odes, students wrote imaginative odes about a treat they would bring in large quantities to share with the class. For example, the sample is "Ode to Chocolate-Covered Ants."

- Although the *list poem* is not addressed directly, many children ended up with lists in their poems. In the beginning of his division ode, William (grade 5) included an exciting list:

Ode to Kittens

. . . I brought in one hundred kittens.
All cute and cuddly,
purring and meowing.
Tan, tabby, and tortoise shell,
Siamese, Persian, Devon Rex.
All kinds of kittens,
all types of cats. . . .

- Many of the math poems that children created could be classified as *free verse* (p. 80), which doesn't rhyme. Free verse often sounds somewhat like natural speech. For example, the estimation poems in which children encounter mother animals in outdoor settings, and estimate the number of babies the mothers have, are written in free verse.

Poetry Tools

Simile

The Poetry Frames in the book also introduce some of the tools poets use. For example, poets often use similes, or comparisons using the words *like* or *as*. Notice the effective use of simile in the addition poem below:

My topic is penguins.
My numbers are 100 + 99

199 Penguins
99 penguins
waddle along.
100 more join them.

Together they
look like friendly goblins.

I shake hands and
we make friends.

Autumn, grade 2

The Poetry Frame for shape riddles prompted the children to write similes. Inez wrote a lovely one.

> . . . *I am as white as a dove*
> **that picks the whitest**
> **flowers with its beak. . . .**
> *Inez, grade 3*

Caitlin brought humor into her poem by using a very funny simile in the fifth line below. This is from her "Ode to Pink Hippos," a division ode.

> . . . **They stampeded the playground**
> **got stuck on the swing**
> **dominated in kickball**
> **and munched on the teachers**
> *like Popsicle sticks.*
> *Caitlin, grade 5*

In their money blues poems, children wrote beautiful similes, such as the one below:

> . . . **I lost my twenty dollar bill.**
> *It's as green as sea grass.*
> *Haleigh, grade 3*

Alliteration

Alliteration, or the repetition of beginning sounds in a poem can make it fun to read. Sara (grade 2) uses the "b" sound over and over, making her poem very satisfying when it's read out loud. It sounds like a swarm of bees.

> My topic is Bees.
> My numbers are 38 + 94

Buzzing Bees
38 buzzing bees fly
inside a hive.
94 join the buzzy bees.

Together they make
a swarming bundle
of bees.

I run home
so I won't get stung.
Sara, grade 2

Tejas has a more subtle alliteration in his estimation poem about finding baby frogs in a pond. Notice the repetition of the "s" sound.

> . . . **I went up a *s*teep hill**
> **trying not to *s*lip on the dew-covered *s*and. . . .** *Tejas, grade 3*

In his estimation poem, Gabriel also used alliteration when talking about a mother turtle.

> . . . She had *four flat flippers*,
> doing all the work. . . .
>
> *Gabriel, grade 3*

Made-up Words

Neologisms are made-up words. In poetry, this is allowed. Paige did a beautiful job of making up a word in her estimation poem about baby spiders—she invented the word *glammering*. She uses alliteration effectively, too, with "d" sounds and "g" sounds.

> . . . One morning as I was walking
> in the *d*amp, *d*ark, wet woods,
> I saw a *g*lammering, *g*littering web
> with a spider in it. . . .
>
> *Paige, grade 3*

Specific Detail

Specific, sensory detail can brighten a poem and draw you in. Kyle used detail that caught my attention in his division poem, an ode to pieces of candy. I could picture the candy in my mind's eye.

> . . . all chewy and sugary
> and covered with bright wrappers. . . .
>
> *Kyle, grade 5*

In her ode to little white mice, Sarah made the mice come alive through detail.

> . . . They scurried from here to there and everywhere,
> their little pink tails dragging behind. . . .
>
> *Sarah, grade 5*

When describing the beagle puppies in his ode, Tasuku included a memorable detail.

> . . . They licked our faces
> as we did our work . . .
>
> *Tasuku, grade 5*

Gabriel used a beautiful detail in his estimation poem about sitting and counting a mother turtle's eggs. He created a picture in the reader's mind.

> . . . I sat down, rested my back
> against a dune . . .
>
> *Gabriel, grade 3*

Rhyme

I don't encourage rhyme because it actually hampers children's creativity, but *internal rhyme* can be delightful. With internal rhyme, the rhyme is within the poem, instead of being at the ends of lines. When Thomas used rhyme in his ode to dog treats, it was very effective.

> . . . **I brought in 145 dog treats**
> **to share with the class,**
> **all crunchy and crispy**
> **all *old* and *moldy*. . . .**

Thomas, grade 5

Paige also used internal rhyme in line four of her blues poem about losing a twenty-dollar bill.

> . . . **Oh, why did I lose it?**
> **Oh, why did I lose it?**
> **That $20 bill so new,**
> **so *clean,* so nice and *green.***
> **Oh, why, Oh, why, Oh, why. . . .**

Paige, grade 3

Lines of Poetry

Lines of poetry are usually shorter than lines of prose. To help children write more poetically, I made the blank lines on the Poetry Frames shorter than usual.

When children are writing, it's best not to bother them about where to break the line. Later, in second drafts, they can think about ending a line where it makes sense—where the thought ends or a natural pause takes place. Below is an example from the beginning of the estimation poem that Katherine wrote:

> . . . **I was walking along the forest path**
> **minding my own business.**
> **I heard crows cawing and birds chirping.**
> **Then I saw a mother frog**
> **staring at me from a pond. . . .**

Katherine, grade 3

Ready to Start

It's time to jump in and try writing math poetry. You can schedule it into your math time or your writing time. You can use it to introduce, practice, or reinforce concepts. It will bring math alive for your poets. It will bring poetry alive for your mathematicians. And it will delight your students who love both.

Yuka Sakazaki

I

Teaching Traditional Math Poetry

100 fish
wiggly, shiny, smooth
10 red, 50 green, 30 blue, 10 yellow
my favorite is the parrotfish
shiny suns sw
across the seas

Teaching traditional math poems can open up mathematics for children. It takes math out of its "box" and makes it whimsical and creative. When teaching traditional math poetry, it is helpful to follow certain steps:

★ Introduce the math topic.

★ Introduce the Poetry Frame through the Sample Poem(s). These can be shown on the overhead or chart paper and/or distributed to children.

★ Show additional sample poems from the Classroom Journal. (optional)

★ Brainstorm ideas for the poems.

★ Write a collaborative poem together, or demonstrate by writing a poem yourself in front of the class. (optional)

★ Pass out the Poetry Frames if you haven't already done so.

★ Encourage each child to pick a topic to help him or her get started.

★ Circulate and give help and encouragement during writing time.

★ Have children revise poems and write final drafts.

★ Invite children to draw pictures to accompany their poems. (optional)

★ Allow children to share their poems, formally or informally.

CHAPTER 1

Number Sense Poems

Sample Poems

100 bees
fuzzy, busy, buzzing
50 are working, 50 are resting
I wish bees didn't sting
100 buzzers

100 fish
wiggly, shiny, smooth
10 red, 50 green. 30 blue, 10 yellow
my favorite is the parrotfish
shiny suns swimming
across the seas

Elizabeth, grade 3

1,000 ants
marching, black, small
each ant has six legs, 6,000 legs in all
streaming like missiles
puny marchers

David, grade 3

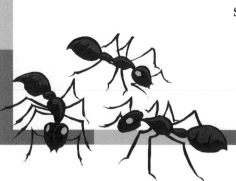

POETRY FRAME
Poems about 100 and Beyond

_____

_____, _____, _____

_____

_____

_____

objects
three   describing   words
something about the objects that has numbers
how   you   feel   about   the   objects
new or same name for the objects

_____

_____, _____, _____

_____

_____

_____

Your Drawing

Name _____

Classroom Journal: Number Sense Poems

My first experience with math poetry was in a third-grade classroom. I introduced a lesson on writing Number Sense Poems, which included the math concepts of number sense, place value, and the operations.

We started by compiling an extensive list of things that are often found in groups of 100 or 1,000. The children were immediately engaged. Their list included spider babies, ants, fish, snowflakes, pennies, and dust mites, which one of the boys was allergic to.

Next, I introduced the Poetry Frame below and told them that they could use it as a springboard. Many children had seen this form, called a *diamanté*. I adjusted it to include numbers in the third line, and I gave the children many examples of how that line could be written. In your classroom, you can use the Sample Poems on page 18 and the children's poems in this Classroom Journal to help your children with line 3.

_____	objects
_____, _____, _____	three describing words
_____	something about the objects that has numbers
_____	how you feel about the objects
_____	new or same name for the objects

Elizabeth had a concerned look on her face when she started, as if there were a certain way to write the poem, which I assured her there wasn't. She was smiling when she finished her elegant poem:

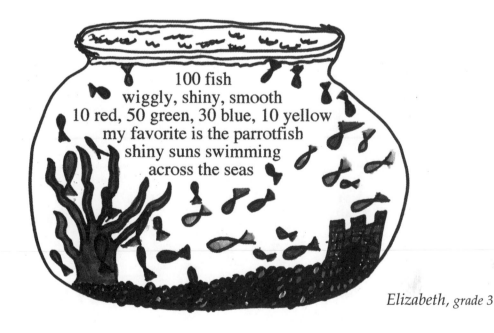

100 fish
wiggly, shiny, smooth
10 red, 50 green, 30 blue, 10 yellow
my favorite is the parrotfish
shiny suns swimming
across the seas

Elizabeth, grade 3

David's sharpness came through in his poem:

> **1,000 ants**
> **marching, black, small**
> **each ant has six legs, 6,000 legs in all**
> **streaming like missiles**
> **puny marchers**
>
> *David, grade 3*

Ben told me he has trouble with handwriting but his creativity, his vast knowledge, and his rich vocabulary were evident:

> **100 jellyfish**
> **upside down, lighting, drifting**
> **50 are electric, 50 are flower-hatted**
> **calm, happy, mysterious**
> **100 stingers**
>
> *Ben, grade 3*

Taylor, who finds spelling and writing a challenge, was very proud of his poem:

> **Stars**
> **Distant, shiny, floating**
> **1,000 stars coming out 1 by 1**
> **If the stars weren't there, it would be dark.**
> **Sparklers**
>
> *Taylor, grade 3*

After the success of my first math poetry workshop, I was off and running.

Teacher Notes: Number Sense Poems

1. Introduce the concept of 100 and 1,000 by brainstorming things that come in quantities of 100 and 1,000. Possibilities include:

ants	fish	dust mites
frogs	jellyfish	pennies
spider babies	penguins	teeth on a shark
gnats	leaves	snowflakes
moles	bees	raindrops

2. Explain the form of the poem—a *diamanté,* or diamond-shaped poem.

_____	objects
_____, _____, _____	three describing words
_____	something about the objects that has numbers
_____	how you feel about the objects
_____	new or same name for the objects

3. Display and/or distribute the Sample Poems.
4. Write a *diamanté* poem together as a class if you think it will help.
5. Have children choose a topic.
6. Circulate as children write and/or illustrate their own poems.

Easier and Harder

To adjust this Poetry Frame for younger children, make it simpler by including the number 100 on the third line. This would be fun for the hundredth day of school.

bees
fuzzy, busy, buzzing
100 bees making honey at the hive
I wish bees didn't sting
buzzers

To make this poetry prompt more challenging for older children, they can include multiplication or fractions in the mathematical line in the middle of the poem.

CHAPTER 2

Shape Riddles

Sample Poems

Short Riddle

I am red.
I am an octagon.
I make cars stop.
What am I?

Interesting Riddle

I am as red as a ripe berry
that the birds pick in winter
against a gloomy winter sky.

I am an octagon with 8 metal sides
all the same length,
and a metal front you can tap
if you leap up high.

I make drivers slow down
and put on the brakes.
Sometimes I hear the brakes
squeak and squeal!
What am I?

Shape Riddles

My riddle is about _____

I am _____ (color)

I am _____ (shape)

I _____ (what it does, used for)

What am I?

I am as _____ as _____ (color)

_____

_____

_____

I _____ (shape—how many
sides and corners)

_____

_____

_____

I _____ (what it is used for
or what it does)

_____

_____

_____

What am I?

Name _____

Classroom Journal: Shape Riddles

For my next foray into math poetry, I decided to try writing math riddles in a third-grade classroom. I called the poems "shape riddles" because I had the children explore geometric shapes all around them, using poetic language.

First I showed a sample, which consisted of two important parts. The riddle on the left is a typical, bare-bones riddle that children have seen before. On the right, I embellished the short riddle to transform it into a poem. I used a comparison called a *simile* ("I am as red as a ripe berry") in the first line and I added concrete, sensory details throughout.

Short Riddle

I am red.
I am an octagon.
I make cars stop.
What am I?

Poetic Riddle

I am as red as a ripe berry
that the birds pick in winter
against a gloomy winter sky.

I am an octagon with 8 metal sides
all the same length,
and a metal front that you can tap
if you leap up high.

I make drivers slow down
and put on the brakes.
Sometimes I hear the brakes
squeak and squeal!
What am I? (stop sign)

Together, we wrote two riddles about a window:

I am clear.
I am a rectangle.
I let the sun in.
What am I?

I am as clear as a glass of water.
I am a rectangle with 4 sides
and 4 corners.

I let the sunshine in
and keep the house
looking bright and shiny.
What am I? (window)

Then the children were ready to write. First they wrote bare-bones riddles, such as Sinclaire's below:

> **I am red, white, and blue.**
> **I have 4 sides.**
> **I wag in the air.**

Then we made the riddles into poetry by adding detail, by fleshing out the images. Here is Sinclaire's second riddle:

> **I am as red as a cherry,**
> **as blue as water,**
> **and as white as a baby polar bear.**
>
> **I am a rectangle**
> **with 4 sides and**
> **4 corners.**
>
> **I wag slowly as**
> **the small children at**
> **school Pledge Allegiance.**
> **What am I? (the U.S. flag)**

Sinclaire, grade 3

Morgan normally writes about battleships, airplanes, and war. This was the first time I'd seen him explore another subject. He was very pleased and suggested that his was a poem, not a riddle.

Mountains

I am as gray as rain clouds,
black as space,
snow as white as
clouds on my big rocky face.

I am a triangle that
has so many curves
I look like the hat of a witch
with a stream that's as small as a ditch.

The climbers that climb me
look like black little dots
returning from lumbering
to warm little cots.

Morgan, grade 3

Leo described the Earth in his riddle:

**I am as colorful
as a rainbow.**

**I am shaped
like a sphere.
I don't have any
sides and corners.**

**I am used
for people living.
The shape, what it does
is it spins.
What am I? (Earth)**

Leo, grade 3

There was a productive buzz in the room as children informally shared their poems with me and with each other. They were very proud of their shape riddles.

Teacher Notes: Shape Riddles

1. Have children brainstorm a list of shapes in their world:

rectangle	**circle**	**triangle**
bed	donut or bagel	pizza slice
paper	letter o	pennant
flag	clock	bike flag
book		

rhombus	**pentagon**	**hexagon**
kite	orb spider web	snowflake
diamond	shield	beehive cell
kitchen or bathroom tiles		

octagon
stop sign

2. Display or distribute the Sample Poem about a stop sign.
3. Write short and long riddles together as a class.
4. Have children write their own riddles.
5. Allow children to share with the class and guess each other's riddles.

Easier or Harder

For an easier version of the Poetry Frame, have children write only a short riddle, but make the first line interesting.

> **I am as red as a strawberry.**
> **I am an octagon.**
> **I make cars stop.**

For a more difficult version, suggest that students write riddles about objects that are geometric solids: rectangular prisms, cones, cylinders, spheres, triangular prisms, and pyramids.

Addition Poems

Sample Poems

> My topic is raindrops.
> My numbers: 27 + 34

61 Raindrops

27 raindrops
plinking and plunking
into the puddle.
34 more raindrops join them.

Together they build up
to a rock-n-rolling storm.

I dash home
soaked to the bone
with my hair plastered
to my head.

> My topic is stars.
> My numbers: 48 + 32

80 Stars

48 stars are flickering.
32 more stars turn on their lights
in the dark of the sky.

Together they make
a jewelry-box of constellations.

I lie down on my back and look up
and my dog looks up, too.

POETRY FRAME
Addition Poems

My topic is _____

My numbers are _____ + _____

Title _____

_____

_____

_____

_____

Together they

_____

_____

I _____

_____

Name _____

Classroom Journal: Addition Poems

I wanted to test math poetry in the second grade to see if it was viable at the primary level. The children were studying addition, so I came up with the idea of writing a poetic word problem.

First I read the poem "12 Polka-Dots" from my book *Counting Our Way to the 100th Day!* (Markgaret K. McElderry Books, 2004). In the poem, the little gecko has 78 spots on her back and 22 on her tail. I asked the children to tell me how many polka-dots she had altogether. They liked the poem and could see how it was a math poem. (Reading this poem is optional.)

Next, we brainstormed things that could come in groups of 20, 30, 40, 50, 60, 70, 80, 90, 100, and so on. I wrote four general topics on the white board: nature and seasons, animals, school, and sports. I wrote each of their ideas under the appropriate topic. Some of the suggestions were leaves, snowflakes, flowers, mice, crabs, wild horses, books, and sleds on a hill.

I read the Sample Poems I had written for this lesson. One is shown below. I wanted them to see the pattern of the Poetry Frame and the type of language I used—interesting language that painted pictures in their minds.

> My topic: stars
> My numbers: 48 + 32

80 Stars

48 stars are flickering.
32 more stars turn on their lights
in the dark of the sky.

Together they make
a jewelry-box of constellations.

I lie down on my back and look up
and my dog looks up, too.

I showed the children how I had picked two things before starting to write: a topic and the numbers I was going to add. I pointed out that I had written these in the box on the top of the page. I also showed them how I added the numbers to create the title. They found a mistake in my adding in the sample, so I corrected it.

We found the phrases "Together they make" and "Together they build up" in the Sample Poems I wrote (see page 29), and I pointed out that I didn't really add my numbers at that point of the poem. Instead, I used interesting description there. For example, in the second poem, I wrote, "Together they make a jewelry-box of constellations."

We looked at my word choice in each sample. They could see how I had painted pictures that they could visualize or hear in their minds.

We noticed that in the last lines I brought *myself* into the poem. I talked about what *I* was doing.

The children moved back to their desks and began filling in the boxes at the tops of their pages with their topic and their numbers. It was a good way to get started. Many used topics from the board but some made up their own.

The variations in the poems that follow are interesting. I was pleased to see that the Sample Poems and the Poetry Frames gave children a framework to feel safe in but also gave them room for individuality.

Michael followed the format, in his simple, quiet poem.

The topic is snowflakes.
My numbers are 30 + 26

56 Snowflakes

30 snowflakes drop
from the sky.
26 more snowflakes
join them.

Together they fall
slowly to the ground.
I played in the snow
where the snowflakes landed.

Michael, grade 2

Paloma wrote a poem about horses. I noticed the language and the repetition in her second verse right away—it was unusual and strong. She also varied the Poetry Frame by including two different addition problems in her first verse.

My topic is horses.
My numbers are 43 + 77

120 Wild Horses

43 horses running
in the wild.
10 of them are gray and
33 are black.
77 join them right now.

Together they run
like wild horses should.
All different colors.
Like wild horses are.

I watched them that day
and I was amazed.
And I watched them
again and again
and again!

Paloma, grade 2

Clara took off on her own wavelength, literally.

My topic is phones.
My numbers are 82 + 64

146 Phones

82 phones ask
What's your name?
64 answer the question.

Together they make
a conversation,
laughing and giggling,
having so much fun.

I decide to do some chattin, too.
Some hippin', hoppin', shoutin'.

Clara, grade 2

Some children worked the whole period quietly and diligently, while others had questions about the Poetry Frame. Some illustrated theirs on the back. Many were excited about their poetic word problems and wanted to show me, and their neighbors, what they had written.

Teacher Notes: Addition Poems

1. Brainstorm a list of things that come in large groups of 20, 30, 40, 50, 60, 70, 80, or 90. List general topics on the board and fit each suggestion into a category. Here are some possibilities:

nature and seasons

leaves
trees
snowflakes
raindrops
kernels of corn
raindrops
fall leaves
cherry blossoms
seeds in a garden
flowers in a garden
veggies in a garden
stars in the sky

animals

penguins
ducks
dolphins
fish
bunnies
zebras in a herd
seagulls on the beach
crabs at the beach
wild horses
migrating birds
ladybugs hibernating
squirrel nuts in the fall
fish eggs
turtle eggs

school

paper
pencils
erasers
kids
words
books
kids on the playground
wheels on the way to school

sports

sleds on a hill
skiers on a hill

2. Read the Sample Poems with the children to introduce the Poetry Frame.
3. Show how I chose my topic and my numbers before even starting the poem. Point out that I added my numbers to create the title.
4. Pass out the Poetry Frames. After children fill in the box at the top of the page, have them write their own addition poems.

5. Encourage children to illustrate their poetic word problems.

6. Have volunteers share their poems with the class.

Easier and Harder

By varying the numbers in the poems, you can make this Poetry Frame easier or more challenging, mathematically.

From *Math Poetry* © Good Year Books. This page may be reproduced for classroom use only by the actual purchaser of the book. www.goodyearbooks.com

CHAPTER 4

Subtraction Poems

Sample Poem

Simple word problem

12 mice are under a bush,
Along comes a snake.
5 mice run away.
How many mice are left? <u>7 mice</u>

Simple word problem made into a poem

Mice and Snake

12 little big-eared mice
are having a party
under the blackberry bush.

Along slithers a baby garter snake,
back and forth on the soft ground.
5 mice scurry away.
How many mice are left?

P O E T R Y   F R A M E
Subtraction Poems

My topic is _____

Simple Word Problem

_____   Tell how many of your little animal.

Along comes _____   Your big animal

_____   How many little animals go away?

How many are left? _____   How many little animals are left?

Interesting Poem

Title _____

_____   Tell how many of your little animal.

_____

Along _____   Your big animal

_____

_____   How many of your little animals
                                go away?

_____

How many are left? _____   How many little animals are left?

Name _____

Classroom Journal: Subtraction Poems

In the second-grade classroom, I continued my exploration of poetic word problems by introducing a Poetry Frame that required subtraction. The children in this class were just beginning word problems, and the teacher, Sarah Newman, said my Poetry Frame was an excellent introduction.

First the children compiled a list of predators and prey, such as birds and a cat, mice and a snake, worms and a bird, bugs and a bat, flies and a frog, a herd of zebras and a lion. The children were totally engaged in this topic. They knew a lot about animals, although I had to politely correct a few inaccuracies.

Next I showed the children how to transform a typical subtraction problem into a poem, using my Sample Poem. Here is the simple word problem I started with:

12 mice are under a bush,
Along comes a snake.
5 mice run away.
How many mice are left? <u>7 mice</u>

Here is my word problem transformed into a poem. I added rich details and used vivid verbs. The children helped me add some of the detail: how the mice looked, what kind of bush, what kind of garter snake, how the mice moved.

Mice and Snake

12 little big-eared mice
are having a party
under the blackberry bush.

Along slithers a baby garter snake,
back and forth on the soft ground.
5 mice scurry away.

How many mice are left?

The teacher announced that they should use their imaginations and have fun—not to worry about anything. If only "word problems" in textbooks could be as intriguing, in language and in narrative, as the children's poems that follow!

First Christopher wrote a typical word problem.

5 cows are eating grass.
Along comes a vampire bat.
4 cows ran away.
How many are left? <u>1 cow</u>

Then he added rich detail and changed his verb. I was amazed by his use of the verb *moseyed.*

Cows and Vampire Bat

**5 chocolate cows eating
very very wet grass.**

**Along flew a vampire bat.
4 cows moseyed away.**

How many are left?   *Christopher, grade 2*

Notice the vivid images Drew created of the fish and the shark below. His verb *scattered* is very strong!

Fishes and Shark

**15 skinny, see-through fish
playing hide and seek
in the deep water.**

**Along swam a greedy hungry
hammer shark.
8 fish scattered away.**

How many are left?   *Drew, grade 2*

Young-Ju used the words *grazing* and *prowling* in an interesting way—as adjectives.

Zebras and Lion

**25 grazing little zebras
are playing in the field.**

**Along comes a prowling
hungry cheetah ready to attack.**

**15 frightened zebras
gallop away.**

How many are left?   *Young-Ju, grade 2*

Young-Ju went on to write a story about the zebras and the lion called "The Lion's Lesson."

This lesson sparked the children's imaginations and opened the door to subtraction word problems, all in one writing activity.

Teacher Notes: Subtraction Poems

1. Introduce subtraction poems by talking about predators and prey, an inherently interesting topic for children. Brainstorm a list together such as the one below.

   mice and snake
   birds and cat
   worms and bird
   bugs and bat
   flies and frog
   zebras and lion
   mongoose and snake
   bugs and spider
   mice and owl

2. Show and/or distribute the Sample Poem.
3. Write a sample with the children to reinforce the Poetry Frame. First write a simple subtraction word problem. Then add rich language, in the form of sensory detail and vivid verbs, to make the problem into a poem.
4. Pass out the Poetry Frames and have children write their own simple word problems and poems.
5. Encourage children to illustrate their poetic word problems.
6. Have children solve their own problems and each other's as well.

Easier and Harder

To make these subtraction word problems mathematically easier or more challenging, have children use smaller or larger numbers.

C H A P T E R 5

Estimation Poems

Sample Poem

Baby Spiders

I hiked through the damp woods one misty morning.
I could hear birds chip-chipping and my own footsteps.
In the underbrush, I spotted spider webs as big as my hand.
A mother spider was sitting near her egg sac,
her spindly legs covered with tiny hairs.
She bounced up and down and peered at me through her six eyes.

"I have about 1,000 babies in my sac,"
the spider mother said.
I sat down near her on a bed of oak leaves and I counted.
"You have exactly 1,268 eggs," I said.
"Happy Mother's Day, spider."

Then I crunched through the pine needles
and made my way back home.

POETRY FRAME
Estimation Poems

Baby _____

I _____

_____

_____

_____

_____

Description of finding animal mother and babies.

_____

* _____

said _____

The mother estimates how many babies or eggs she has.

I _____

** _____

You count exactly how many babies or eggs.

_____

You make a comment to her and leave.

_____

_____

Name _____

Classroom Journal: *Estimation Poems*

It was a challenge to think of a poetry form for estimation. It was near Mother's Day and I remembered that some animals have large numbers of eggs/babies so I used that as the basis of my Sample Poem.

I did quite a bit of research beforehand about the numbers of eggs/babies certain animals had. That way, when the children were brainstorming, I could verify the facts they contributed.

I introduced the topic and found that children were very knowledgeable. Children and animals go together like bees and honey. On the white board, I quickly sketched the animals they suggested and wrote an estimate of how many babies/eggs each animal had. We talked a little about where they lived as well. When I was sketching, I separated the animals into two groups: those that could have more than 1,000 babies and those that lived in large communities in which there were more than 1,000 babies altogether. For example, each bat has one baby, but there can be thousands of baby bats in the nursery.

By the time we were done, we had statistics about the babies/eggs of bees, ants, shrimp, spiders, and beetles. We also included data on bats, frogs, and penguins.

Some animals that the children named—seahorses and snakes—do not have thousands of offspring. In fact, seahorse dads lay hundreds of eggs, and snakes can lay as many as 50 eggs. Turtles don't lay thousands of eggs either, but I forgot to check my notes so some children used impossibly high numbers for their turtle poems. That was my fault, and we corrected it later. In fact, turtles can lay about 200 to 300 eggs.

Before the children started writing, I introduced my Sample Poem by explaining that a mother spider could have thousands of eggs in her sac. I asked how many children liked spiders and how many didn't—it was about half and half. We reviewed the five senses, and I told them to listen for the senses in my poem. They were very quiet while I read.

I described the assignment as having three parts: a description of meeting the mother, a conversation with her, and an ending. I emphasized that they leave the mother and baby undisturbed at the end of the poem. I encouraged them to create a sense of the place they found the mother animal by using the senses in their descriptions.

Baby Spiders

Description (with Sensory Detail)

I hiked through the damp woods one misty morning.
I could hear birds chip-chipping and my own footsteps.

In the underbrush, I spotted spider webs as big as my hand.
A mother spider was sitting near her egg sac,
her spindly legs covered with tiny hairs.
She bounced up and down and peered at me through her six eyes.

Conversation
"I have about 1,000 babies in my sac,"
the spider mother said.
I sat down near her on a bed of oak leaves and I counted.
"You have exactly 1,268 eggs," I said.
"Happy Mother's Day, spider."

Ending
Then I crunched through the pine needles
and made my way back home.

Before they started to write, we did preliminary work. I asked them to choose an animal and to write the name of the animal in the title. I had them decide *exactly* how many baby animals there were in the poem and to write that number on the *second* blank line on the Poetry Frame (next to the **). Then I had them round that number to the nearest thousand or hundred and write it in the *first* blank line on the Poetry Frame (next to the *).

As the children were writing, the teacher, Alice Anne Chandler, said, "We're having fun with this." The results proved her right. The children did a wonderful job of writing beautiful, moody descriptions and of gently including themselves in the scene with the mother animal.

Katherine put herself in the scene in a lovely way, using the senses of hearing and sight:

I was walking along the forest path
minding my own business.
I heard crows cawing and birds chirping.
Then I saw a mother frog
staring at me from a pond.   *Katherine, grade 3*

Tejas painted a picture. You could almost feel the slippery sand.

I went up a steep hill
trying not to slip on the dew-covered sand.
I found a pond with trees around it.
There were many frogs inside.   *Tejas, grade 3*

Their conversations with the animal were more friendly, thoughtful, and personal than mine had been, and I loved that. This is evident in Paige's poem:

Baby Bees

I walked by a pond
on a foggy morning in spring.
When I stopped, I saw a bee's nest.
"Hello, hello," I hollered in.
A bee came out.

"I think I have 2,000 babies,"
said the bee.
"I will count for you," I said.

I sat down and started to count.
I got to 2,000.
"You have 2,004, " I said,
counting the last 4.
"Good luck with the babies," I said,
and quietly and calmly and slowly
I made my way home.

Paige, grade 3

Some children understood the point of the estimation in the poem more than others, but most gave it quite a bit of thought. Frankie made his poem interesting by using a very large number:

Baby Shrimp

I went scuba diving one day
and I found some shrimp.
They were tiny and had a hard shell
to protect themselves.

"I have about 400,000,"
said mommy shrimp.

I counted exactly 400,564 babies.

"Good luck with all those babies.
Bye."

Frankie, grade 3

I was pleased to find that some students were interested in doing research. Katherine didn't want to write about thousands of eggs in a pond. She wanted to find out how many eggs one frog would lay. I suggested she look it up in the encyclopedia. She found out that frogs lay several hundred eggs and used that fact when she was writing.

The most amazing transformation happened with Alex. He came up and told me that sea turtles only come onto the sand when they are born and that when they have babies, they spend most of their time in the water. Then he showed me his poem, which was very moving. I said, "Alex, you must like to write," implying that he was a good writer. "No I don't like to write," he replied with conviction. He couldn't explain why, but he said he didn't mind writing this poem. We both agreed it was the best thing he'd ever written. His teacher, Alice Anne Chandler, was thrilled with this breakthrough, because that's precisely what it was for him.

Baby Turtles

I was walking
through the soft sand.
I could hear the waves
crashing on the sea.

I was walking back.
I saw a turtle and it said,
"I just laid 300 eggs."

I looked in her hole and
I counted 284 eggs.

I was just going to say good-bye
but she had already gone back
in the salty ocean sea.

Alexander, grade 3

Ryan's poem showed lovely imagery along with a sense of humor. Calling the bats "nurses" and "nurser bats" added humor to the poem.

Baby Bats

I hiked through the mountains
one cloudy morning.
I could hear rocks crunching.
In a cave I could hear bats squeaking.

"We have about 2,000 in our nursery,"
said one of the nurses.

I sat on a rock and counted.
They had exactly 2,387.

"Happy Mother's Day, nurser bat," I said.
Then I followed the path
back down to the bottom.

Ryan, grade 3

I left that third-grade classroom feeling very satisfied. The children's poems showed a delightful intersection of research, math, and poetry.

Teacher Notes: *Estimation Poems*

1. Introduce estimation poems by talking about animals or communities of animals that have more than 1,000 babies/eggs at one time. Brainstorm a list together. Sketch, or have students sketch, the animal next to the number of offspring, if you're so inclined. It might be helpful to separate the animals, as I have done, into those that individually have many offspring and communities of animals with many offspring.

Animals That Have Many Offspring

Bees: The queen bee lays about 2,000 eggs a day in spring.

Ants and termites: The queen lays thousands of eggs. Ant babies are cared for in the nursery underground. Ants are found all over, in the meadow, in the desert, in the mountains, at the seashore. But they are not found in Antarctica.

Shrimp: Shrimp babies are found in the ocean. One shrimp can lay 500,000 eggs.

Spiders: Spiders can have thousands of eggs in their egg sacs. Spiders can be found in woods, in meadows, in backyards, in garages, and in many other habitats.

Beetles: One beetle can lay 2,000 to 3,000 eggs.

Animals That Live in Communities Where There Are Many Offspring

Bats: Inside a bat colony, each female bat has one baby bat, but all the babies are cared for in a nursery inside the bat cave. There could be thousands or millions of babies in the nursery.

Frogs: A pond or lake can have thousands of tadpoles laid by many different frogs. One frog can lay 100 to 200 eggs.

Penguins: Most penguins lay 2 eggs; some lay 1. But in a rookery, there can be thousands of penguin eggs altogether.

2. Display and/or distribute the Sample Poem to introduce the Poetry Frame. Have children note the three parts: the descriptive beginning with references to the five senses, the conversation, and the ending.

3. Pass out the Poetry Frames. Have children choose an animal and write it in the title. Have children write in the exact number of offspring on the blank with two stars. On the blank with one star, have children round their number to hundreds or thousands place.

4. Encourage children to illustrate their poetry.

5. Allow children to share their work.

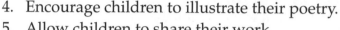

Easier or Harder

Younger children can use smaller numbers for the number of babies. Or they can use animals that have smaller numbers of babies. For example, alligators can lay about 50 to 60 eggs, snakes can lay 40 to 50 eggs, frogs lay about 100 to 200 eggs, and turtles lay about 200 to 300 eggs. (Note that these are maximum numbers.) Older children should work carefully with their numbers in the poem, making sure that the number of offspring is rounded correctly to the hundreds or thousands place.

CHAPTER 6

Money Blues Poems

Sample Poem

Singing the Money Blues

Oh, why did I lose my $20 bill?
Oh, why did I lose my $20 bill?
As green as algae in a new spring pond,
with a wide-winged eagle spreading its wings,
and jazzy fonts all over, like some cool poster.

Oh, what I could have bought with my $20 bill.
Oh, what I could have bought with my $20 bill.
   2 honey-colored goldfish for $3 each,
   2 see-through yo-yos for $6 each,
   with $2 left over for my piggy bank.

Oh, why did I drop it down that grate?
Oh, why did I drop it down that grate?
Now all I can do is sing the money blues.

POETRY FRAME
Money Blues Poems

Title _____

_____ Complain

_____ Describe

_____

_____

_____ Complain

_____ What could you have
bought?

_____

_____

_____ Complain about what
happened to your $20.

_____

Now, _____

Name _____

Classroom Journal: Money Blues Poems

Writing money poems started out with a bang in a third-grade classroom. Children were intrigued when I passed out an enlarged photocopy of the back and front of a new twenty-dollar bill to each pair of students. (It's okay to photocopy money if you enlarge the bill 150% or more, or reduce it 75% or more.) We talked about the old and the new twenty-dollar bill, and about how you can put a new dollar bill up to the window and see lots of images. We were fascinated to find small *20s* all over the back of the bill. They showed up clearly on the photocopy; on the bill, they looked gold.

Our first task was to create a discount store that we named "The Store." We brainstormed items that were under ten dollars to stock the store. We included toys, pets, drawing materials, knickknacks, and food. (See page 55.)

I explained that we would be writing blues poems about money. One child volunteered that a blues poem was a poem about something sad. I agreed and I added that it could be a poem in which the poet complains or moans about something difficult or disappointing. When I explained that they would be writing a poem about losing their twenty-dollar bill, they all groaned (because they were attached to their photocopied twenty-dollar bills), and we laughed.

Then I read my sample poem with expression. My sample helped them understand the format and the tone or mood of a traditional blues poem. I pointed out the repetition in the first two lines and throughout the poem. We agreed that when something goes wrong, we often say it over and over again, "Oh, why did that happen? Why did that happen?" I explained that Langston Hughes, who wrote many blues poems and helped develop blues poetry, often made some slight variation in his repeated lines. For example, I could have said,

> **Oh, why did I have to lose my $20 bill?**
> **Oh, why in the world did I have to lose my $20 bill?**

I broke down my poem (see page 52) into three parts for them. The first part complains that I lost my twenty-dollar bill and describes what it looked like and what was so cool about how it looked. The second part complains about all the things I could have bought with it. This part involves the math. The third part tells how I lost the twenty-dollar bill.

Singing the Money Blues

Complaining that I lost the bill
Oh, why did I lose my $20 bill?
Oh, why did I lose my $20 bill?

Describing how cool it looked
As green as algae in a new spring pond,
with a wide-winged eagle spreading its wings,
and jazzy fonts all over, like some cool poster.

Complaining about what I could have bought
Oh, what I could have bought with my $20 bill.
Oh, what I could have bought with my $20 bill.
   2 honey-colored goldfish for $3 each,
   2 see-through yo-yos for $6 each,
   with $2 left over for my piggy bank.

Telling how I lost it
Oh, why did I drop it down that grate?
Oh, why did I drop it down that grate?
Now all I can do is sing the money blues.

For the second part, the math part, the children copied my format in which I named the prices of things I'd purchased and told how much money would have been left over. Not everyone did this in the first draft, but I had them go back and revise if they didn't. Also, if I presented the Poetry Frame again, I would tell the children that they needed to buy 2 or 3 of something, when reasonable, to involve them in multiplication. (For example, they don't need two skateboards, but they could buy two goldfish or two bean bag animals.)

Someone asked if they had to use only the items we had listed in the store. I said, "No way." They asked if they could start their poems with the same words I used. I said "Yes, but if you can think of your own words, that would be even better." It turned out that for some children, using my first sentence was a way to get into their poem. I also noticed that some followed the three-part format I had modeled, while others didn't. For example, some told how they lost the bill in the first verse. I welcomed these variations.

When the children started writing, everyone was engaged. The topic really tickled them. Their poems ended up being little sagas about a lost twenty-dollar bill, each with its own dramatic story line. I figured out that students are very good at complaining, so when told to write a blues poem, they really go for it. The poems were funny, beautiful, poignant, and dramatic.

Paige has a very natural style, with poetic touches throughout:

Singing the Money Blues

Oh, why did I lose it?
Oh, why did I lose it?
That $20 bill so new,
so clean, so nice and green.
Oh, why, Oh, why, Oh, why.

Oh, what I could buy.
Oh, what I could do.
    I could get 2 packs
    of candy for 2 bills each,
    5 rubber bracelets for $1 each,
    and a stuffed bear for $7,
    and even a fish.

I think my room lost it.
Now, I can't buy anything
and I can't do anything
except look for that $20 bill.

Paige, grade 3

Gabriel was very dramatic in his language.

Singing the Money Blues

Oh, why did I lose my $20 bill?
Oh, why did it fly away?
As green as the sea,
with writing all over it,
and cool Mr. Jackson on the front.

Oh, what I could have with my $20 bill.
Oh, what I could have.
1 skateboard for $9,
2 flashlights $7 each,
and a bag of goldfish for $4.

Oh, why did it fly out of my grasp?
Oh, why did it part from ME?
Now, all I can do is sing the money blues.

Gabriel, grade 3

Katherine's poem shows off her flowing style of writing:

Singing the Money Blues

Oh, why did I lose that $20 bill?
Oh, why did I lose that $20 bill?
As green as grass on a fine spring day,
with the White House neatly drawn on the back,
and a smiling president, looking up at me.

Oh, what I would have bought with that $20 bill.
Oh, there are lots I could buy with that $20 bill.
 2 paperback books for $5 each,
 2 cool key chains for $3 each,
 with $9 left to put in my bank.

Oh, why did I show it to that dog.
Oh, why did that dog chew it up.
Now, all I can do is go on home.   *Katherine, grade 3*

Each one of the children drew me into the narrative of their compelling blues poems. Everyone listened attentively when the children shared completed poems with the class.

Teacher Notes: Money Blues Poems

1. Introduce money poems by passing out or displaying an enlarged twenty-dollar bill, back and front. Discuss the appearance of the bill.

2. Create a discount store on the board or chart paper. Have children stock it with items that are under ten dollars, such as those shown below:

THE STORE			
Sale			
computer game	$8	bean bag animal	$5
skateboard	$9	sticker	$3
keychain	$3	book	$5
stuffed bear	$7	rubber bracelet	$1
candy	$2	markers	$6
goldfish	$4	paint brush	$4
mouse	$8	pet rock	$2
frog	$9	flashlight	$7
		watch	$2

Students thought up food prices on their own.

3. Explain what a blues poem is and tell the children that they are going to write a blues poem about losing a twenty-dollar bill.

4. Display or distribute the Sample Poem. Read it out loud. Point out the repetitions. Explain that those repetitions can vary a little.

5. Talk about the three-part structure of the poem: a complaint and a description of the bill, a complaint about what they could have bought with the bill, and an explanation of how the bill got lost.

6. Point out the simile in the first verse of the sample poem: "As green as algae in a spring pond." Explain that a simile compares two different things that have something in common, using the words *like* or *as*.

7. Pass out the Poetry Frames and have children write their own money blues. Invite them to use interesting words when describing the bill. Have them follow the format in the second verse of the Sample Poem, the part about what they could buy. Encourage them to buy more than one of each item they choose and to tell how much money is left over.

8. Invite children to illustrate their poems.

9. Give children time to share their poems with the class.

Easier or Harder

Younger children could "lose" a five-dollar bill. Older children could "lose" a fifty-dollar bill, and the items in the store could include dollars and cents.

CHAPTER 7

Measurement Poems

Sample Poem

Right now I am 122 centimeters tall.
That's 1 meter and 22 centimeters.

If I Were 10 Centimeters Tall

If I were only 10 centimeters tall,
I'd slide down a pencil. .... 15 cm
I'd take a nap in someone's pocket. .... 16 cm deep
I'd boogie down the white-board tray. .... 7 meters

But I'd watch out for fourth graders .... about 120 cm tall
with giant feet that could stomp me flat. .... about 24 cm
I'd stay away from the curvy slide .... 3 meters
on the playground, too.
I'd land upside-down at the bottom, for sure.

But honestly, it would be great fun
if I were 10 centimeters tall.

Best of all,
I would ride my beagle Sammy to school. .... 50 cm

POETRY FRAME
Measurement Poems

Right now I am _____ centimeters tall.
That's _____ meter and _____ centimeters.

If I Were 10 Centimeters Tall

If I were only 10 centimeters tall, *(tell fun things below)*

I'd _____   _____

   _____   _____

I'd _____   _____

   _____   _____

I'd _____   _____

   _____   _____

I'd watch out for *(tell troublesome things below)*

   _____   _____

   _____   _____

   _____   _____

   _____   _____

But honestly, it would be great fun
if I were 10 centimeters tall.

(tell the most fun thing you could do)
Best of all, I'd _____

   _____

Name _____

Classroom Journal: Measurement Poems

The third-grade class I visited had spent several weeks measuring in centimeters and meters prior to my workshop. Before the session started, the teacher passed out centimeter rulers and made meter sticks available.

I told the children they were going to write a poem about what would happen if they were only 10 centimeters tall. They thought it was funny when we used our centimeter rulers and spread our fingers to show how tall 10 cm is. I showed with my fingers how little they would be if they stood on a desk or on the floor. Someone suggested that Stuart Little might have been that tall.

The teacher had warned me she didn't have time to have them measure playground equipment in meters. So I brought in some playground data that I had rounded to the nearest meter: heights of basketball hoops, lengths of slides, and measurements relating to the monkey bars.

The first thing the children did was measure each other in pairs and record their heights at the top of the poem. This gave them some benchmarks, and some practice measuring.

Then I read the sample poem, along with the measurements to the right of the sample poem. I explained that when they were writing their poems, they would need to open their imaginations. Reading the helpful questions below assisted them in generating fresh ideas.

Helpful Questions
Where could you hide?
What things could you play on in the classroom?
What things could you play on outside the classroom?
How would you get to school?
What would you use for paper and pencil?
What would you eat for lunch?
What would you use for a bed?
What might be dangerous, inside and outside the classroom?
What would you have to be careful of?
What is the most fun thing you could do?

Some children wrote the imaginative part first and then did the measuring and recording. Others did both at once. They interacted quite a bit and got pleasure from each other's ideas and from the humor in each other's poems. Even when I said they didn't need to fill every line, most children insisted on filling the whole page.

Sometimes the children measured exactly. Sometimes they estimated by looking at their centimeter rulers or meter sticks, or by using prior measurements they had taken as benchmarks. I didn't expect them to be involved in so much estimation, but it made sense because they were often writing about objects that weren't physically in the room. For example, Albert asked how far it would be if he fell from the monkey bars, and we used the meter sticks to come up with an estimate of 2 meters. Other children estimated the length of remote control cars, of real cars, of the ceiling lights, of street drains, and more.

They were so involved in measuring that Steven measured a long table just for fun. He also helped me correct my estimate of the length of the white-board tray in my poem.

Some poems had more examples than others. Both short and long poems were effective. Frankie really stretched his imagination and used interesting language, especially in his second verse.

If I Were 10 Centimeters Tall

I'd stick myself on a computer
and pretend I'm in a computer game.   25 cm
I'd skateboard off rulers.   30 cm
I'd ride on birds to get to school.

I'd watch out for   25 cm
feet of big humongous people
that could squash me silly
and gusts of strong wind.

But honestly, I'd have a ton of fun
if I were 10 centimeters tall.

Best of all, I'd bungee jump off desks.   63 cm

Frankie, grade 3

Aaron's was very clever, particularly the ending.

If I Were 10 Centimeters Tall

I'd swim with my pet fish.   23 cm
I'd use lead for a pencil. $\frac{1}{2}$ cm
I'd make a cardboard house.   60 cm

I'd watch out for
bouncing balls,   22 cm

trucks on the road,	1,000 cm or 10 m
hail balls falling,	2 cm
being stuck in people's pockets,	3 cm
and almost drowning in the washer.	

But honestly, it would be fun
if I were 10 centimeters tall.

Best of all, I'd be the best one at hide and seek.

Aaron, grade 3

Albert only wrote about the perils of being 10 cm tall. His poem had a twist at the end!

If I Were 10 Centimeters Tall

If I were only 10 centimeters tall,	
I'd have trouble reading humongous books.	30 cm
I'd be so small I can't reach the doorknob to get in.	60 cm
I'd watch out for soccer balls at recess.	23 cm
I'd watch out for 4th graders who might think I'm a baseball	
and throw me through a classroom window.	360 cm
I'd have to carry a parachute because I might fall	
from the monkey bars.	180 cm

But honestly, I would be having a dream
if I were 10 centimeters tall.

Best of all, I'd wake up! *Albert, grade 3*

The children had a lot of fun using their imaginations and springboarding off each other's ideas. There was also a lot of significant measuring and estimating going on throughout the workshop.

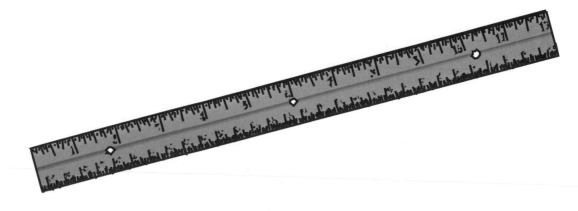

Teacher Notes: Measurement Poems

1. Pass out the Poetry Frames and the Sample Poem, or show the Sample Poem on the overhead or chart paper. Pass out centimeter rulers and make meter sticks available.

2. Explain that children will be writing poems about being only 10 cm tall.

3. Have children show how high 10 cm is with their fingers.

4. Read the Sample Poem and the helpful questions.

5. List the measurements below from a generic playground (if they haven't already measured the playground equipment prior to the lesson).

   ▶ basketball hoops
     medium basketball hoop is about 2 m
     high basketball hoop is about 3 m

   ▶ slides
     kindergarten slide is about 1 m 80 cm, or 180 cm
     tunnel slide is about 3 m
     curvy slide is about 3 m

   ▶ monkey bars
     bars are about 30 cm apart
     length of all the bars is about 3 m

6. Go over the Poetry Frame. Talk about the title of the poem ("If I Were 10 Centimeters Tall") and invite children to brainstorm some fun things they might do, some things that would be hard to do, and some things that they would have to watch out for, if they were only 10 cm high. Encourage children to use their imaginations. Anything goes!

7. Recommend that children save their best idea for the last line of the poem.

8. Remind them to fill in the measurements in the blanks on the right of the page.

9. Invite them to illustrate their poems if they have time.

10. Let children share their poems with the class.

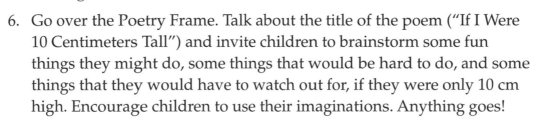

Easier and Harder

For younger children, you can use inches or nonstandard units of measurement. For older children, you can have them measure to the nearest tenth of a centimeter.

CHAPTER 8

Multiplication Poems

Sample Poems

Skateboard wheels come in 4s.
When 5 of us scooter down the sidewalk,
whipping along like the wind,
20 wheels sound like a hive of quiet bees.

Since arms come in twos,
quintuplets have 10.
10 arms for throwing,
and waving to friends.

8 legs on a spider.
Another one comes along.
3 more spider robbers come.
Now all 5 spiders together have 40 legs.

Inez, grade 3

POETRY FRAME

Multiplication Poems

My topic is _____

_____

_____

_____

_____

My topic is _____

_____

_____

_____

_____

Name _____

Classroom Journal: Multiplication Poems

Of course, multiplication is very important in third grade. The teacher in the classroom I visited, Alice Anne Chandler, who loves poetry, was delighted that the children were combining poetry and multiplication practice during the regular writing time.

The children and I started by brainstorming things that come in twos, threes, fours, fives, and on up to twelves. This was lots of fun even though they had done it before.

I passed out a copy of my Sample Poems to each child, and read them out loud. At that point, I asked the children to choose a topic, because the act of choosing a topic can get children started. I suggested that they pick something they liked, or cared about, or knew something about. I was surprised to find that they really challenged themselves—they wrote more complicated poetry than mine. But as complex as their poems were, these young poets never had trouble keeping track of the numbers in the situations they created.

Inez's poem is extraordinary as a poem in itself. The image of "spider robbers" is very imaginative and very descriptive of spiders in the night.

8 legs on a spider,
another one comes by.
Night to midnight,
3 spider robbers come.
Now all the spiders together
have 40 legs.

Inez, grade 3

Ruby revealed her sense of humor:

> **One elephant has 4 legs.**
> **If you have 3 other elephants**
> **16 legs would make**
> **a stampede!**   *Rubi, grade 3*

Emily's has a simile, a comparison of two things with the word *like*:

> **Twins come in 2s**
> **so 4 legs all together.**
> **When they're both**
> **kicking the ball**
> **4 legs kicking like donkeys.**   *Emily, grade 3*

Dulce, an ELL student, created a beautiful, haunting poem:

> **4 feet on a dog**
> **and two more come along**
> **and now all 12 feet**
> **sing a sad song.**   *Dulce, grade 3*

Teacher Notes: Multiplication Poems

1. Brainstorm objects that come in twos, threes, fours, and so on up to twelves.

twos	threes	fours	fives
• bicycle wheels • ears • hands • scooter wheels • chopsticks	• triplets • singers in a trio • tricycle wheels • sides on a triangle • tennis balls in a can	• cat legs • skateboard wheels • quadruplets • stomachs in a cow • quarters in a dollar	• starfish arms • fingers • quintuplets • toes on a foot • pennies in a nickel • senses
sixes	**sevens**	**eights**	**nines**
• insect legs • sodas in a pack • vowels • strings on a guitar	• rainbow colors • days in a week	• spider legs • octopus legs • crab legs	• positions on a baseball field • squares in a hopscotch grid • innings in a baseball game
tens	**elevens**	**twelves**	
• fingers • toes • pins in bowling • dimes in a dollar	• positions in soccer	• eggs in a carton • months in a year	

2. Show or distribute the Sample Poems.
3. Write a class poem about animal legs or another popular topic.
4. Encourage each child to pick a topic to write about and to share with a neighbor.

5. Have children write and illustrate their own multiplication poems.
6. Give children time to share their work with the class.

Easier and Harder

By using smaller or larger numbers, you can make these poems easier or more challenging, from a mathematical point of view.

Lena Latour

CHAPTER 9

Division Odes

Sample Poem

Ode to Chocolate Covered Ants

I brought in 130 chocolate-covered ants
to share with the class,
all crunchy and munchy
and covered with smooth milk chocolate.

They melted in our mouths
and crawled down our throats
and made us all antsy all day.

With 21 in the class,
we each got 6 of them,
with 4 left over for Ms. Mason.

What a treat my chocolate-covered ants were!
What a creepy-crawly treat!

$$21\overline{)130} \quad \begin{array}{r} 6 \ \ \text{R }4 \\ \hline \end{array}$$
$$\underline{-126}$$
$$4$$

P O E T R Y   F R A M E
Division Odes

Ode to _____

I brought in _____   (Tell how many.)

_____

_____

_____

_____

_____

_____

With _____ in the class _____   (How many in the class?)

we each got _____ of them,   (How many for each?)

with ____ left over for _____ .   (How many left over?)

What a treat my _____ were!

What a _____ treat!

Name _____

Classroom Journal: Division Odes

The fifth-grade class I visited had studied long division for two weeks by the time I arrived. The lesson worked like a charm.

First I asked the students if they knew what an ode was. Carly said it was a poem in praise of something. I agreed, and I went on to explain that an ode tells lots of good things about a person or a topic. For example, if you made an ode to your teacher, it would include all of the things you like about her or him. An ode to summer would include all of the wonderful things about summer.

I explained that I'd written an ode to chocolate-covered ants, and I read my Sample Poem, which they thought was funny. Next I told them that they were going to pick something to "bring" to the class to share with their classmates, as I had. I explained that they were going to write an ode to whatever they had chosen to bring in. They were pleased when I told them it could be fun, funny, odd, gross (but not too gross), magical, ridiculous, delicious, and so on. It could create a chaotic or fun or beautiful atmosphere in the classroom—whatever they wanted. I encouraged them to use their imaginations.

We brainstormed ideas for their poems. I had a list with the following items to prime their pumps: chocolate-covered ants, jellybeans, shells, sparkly beads, videogame tokens, pumpkin seeds, paperback books, ladybugs, sauteed snails, and magic beans. When someone added hamsters to the list, we all had fun picturing that. That sparked many more ideas about animals, small and large. The students asked if the scene they created had to make logical sense. The answer was no.

There were some rules though. In the poem, the number of students in the class, or classes, had to be a two-digit number, and the number of items they brought in had to be more than 100 (between 100 and 999). The other suggestion was that they avoid brand names.

Caitlin came up with a wild poem that was delightfully imaginative.

Ode to Pink Hippos

I brought in 107 pink hippos to school
to share with all the girls and boys.
They always raised their hand
but when it came to recess . . .

They stampeded the playground
got stuck on the swing

dominated in kickball
and munched on the teachers
like Popsicle sticks.

With 19 in the class
we each got 5 of them,
with 12 left over for the next class over.

What a treat my pink hippos were!
What an awful mistake was my treat!

Caitlin, grade 5

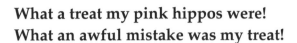

$$19 \overline{)107} \quad \begin{array}{c} 5 \quad \text{R } 12 \\ \end{array}$$
$$\begin{array}{r} -95 \\ \hline 12 \end{array}$$

Tasuku wrote an ode that was very appealing. The teacher, Gaelyn Mason, said it boosted his confidence, as it should have.

Ode to Beagle Puppies

I brought in 100 beagle puppies
to share with my class,
all cute and cuddly
and new and clean.

They licked our faces
as we did our work
and we got off the subject
and our teacher got mad.

With 21 in the class
we each got 4 of them,
with 16 left over for Ms. Mason.

What a treat my Beagle puppies were!
What a cute treat!

Tasuku, grade 5

$$21 \overline{)100} \quad \begin{array}{c} 4 \quad \text{R } 16 \\ \end{array}$$
$$\begin{array}{r} -84 \\ \hline 16 \end{array}$$

Fantasy came into play in Emma's poem:

Ode to Magic Beans

**I brought in 215 magic beans
to share in the class
all tickling in our mouths
and prickly to our skin.**

**Soon there were things
all over the room—wishing teapots,
and growling bears.
What a fun day!**

**With 21 in the class
we each got 10 of them,
with 5 left over for the class hamster.**

**What a treat my magic beans were!
What a magical treat!**

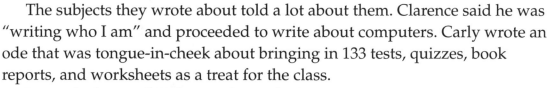

Emma, grade 5

$$21\overline{)215} \quad \begin{array}{r} 10 \ \ \text{R } 5 \\ \hline 215 \\ -210 \\ \hline 5 \end{array}$$

The subjects they wrote about told a lot about them. Clarence said he was "writing who I am" and proceeded to write about computers. Carly wrote an ode that was tongue-in-cheek about bringing in 133 tests, quizzes, book reports, and worksheets as a treat for the class.

I got a kick out of William, who tricked me in order to avoid complicated long division. In his poem, he brought in 100 kittens and divided them among 99 people. The answer was 1 each with 1 left over!

It was the students' idea to read aloud for the class. They took turns and spontaneously clapped for each other's poems. Tasuku, who wrote the charming ode about beagle puppies, was the first to volunteer, which the teacher said was unusual for him.

What a successful workshop! I didn't want to leave and they didn't want me to leave either.

Teacher Notes: Division Odes

1. Explain to students that an ode is in praise of something. Tell them that they're going to be writing some silly odes and doing some division in their odes.

2. Read the Sample Poem to the students to introduce the Poetry Frame. Explain that they need to pick something to share with the class (in their poem only).

3. Tell them the rules about the numbers in their poems: They need to bring in at least 100 treats. The number of class members needs to be a two-digit number.

4. Pass out or display the Sample Poem and distribute the Poetry Frames. Look at the poem together to discover that the beginning tells all the wonderful things about the item. Then there's the part where the treats are divided up. Then there are two lines of praise at the end.

5. Have the students write their own division odes, doing their division work on the bottom of the page.

6. Encourage students to illustrate their poems if they have time.

7. Have students share their poems with the class. I guarantee this will be fun.

Easier and Harder

You can adjust this poem up or down by varying the number of items to be divided and the number of people in the class or group.

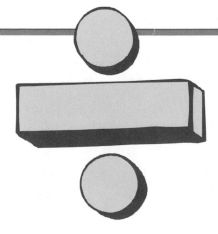

CHAPTER 10

Fractions of Me Poems

Sample Poem

Fractions of Me

$\frac{2}{6}$ of me is a poet:
Inside my mind,
skies, seas, people, beasts
swirl around waiting to be picked
for the next poem.

$\frac{1}{6}$ of me is a mother
with 3 sons, grown and gone,
a mother mostly by cell or e-mail.

$\frac{1}{6}$ of me glides through
the turquoise water,
pedals with the wind in my ears:
a swimmer and a biker.

$\frac{2}{6}$ of me is a wife
hiking down creek beds
where mountain lions have been.

All the 6ths of me
$\frac{2}{6} + \frac{1}{6} + \frac{1}{6} + \frac{2}{6}$
make a whole.

The whole me.

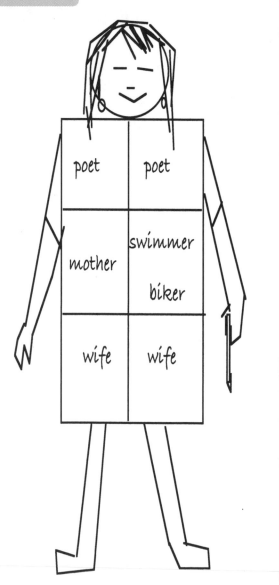

POETRY FRAME

Fractions of Me Poems

Fractions of Me

_____

_____

_____

_____

_____

_____

_____

_____

_____

_____

_____

_____

_____

_____

_____

_____

_____

_____

_____

Name _____

Classroom Journal: Fractions of Me Poems

I introduced the Poetry Frame "Fractions of Me" to a fourth-grade class, even though the students hadn't yet explored fractions deeply with their teacher.

I spent some time going over my Sample Poem on the overhead. First I filled in the picture of my body with the "fractions of me." We talked about the fraction of me that was a poet ($\frac{2}{6}$), a mother ($\frac{1}{6}$), an athlete ($\frac{1}{6}$), and a wife ($\frac{2}{6}$). Then we added all the fractions. The students said it added up to a whole, but we needed to discuss that a whole is equal to $\frac{6}{6}$.

Then I drew in my face and hair to show what I looked like. I also drew in my limbs in a way that indicated that I was a writer—I put a pencil in my hand.

Next, I read my poem, emphasizing the fact that I included specific details that were intriguing. A few of the students related to the fact that my mind was filled with a world of "skies, seas, people, and beasts." I told them I was glad I wasn't alone.

Once the Poetry Frames were distributed, I enumerated the steps they should take: First they were to fill in their interests in the squares on the "Poetry Frame person." I suggested that they could think about how they spend their time, what they like to do, their role in the family, what they think about, and any other relevant personal information. Second, they could draw themselves. Third, they should write the poem. I reminded them not to forget the end of the poem, where all the fractions are added.

Some students surprised me by their interests and what they spent their time thinking about. Because they were very invested in representing themselves accurately, they didn't want to just write in anything. Everyone gave a great deal of thought to their responses. I learned more about the students that day than ever before. It was eye-opening for the teacher, too.

For example, Kelly wrote about her passion:

> $\frac{2}{6}$ of me is an equestrian.
> I dream about horses.
> I love them, and learn about them
> in my dreams.
> I ride all the time.

Sinclaire described her interest in dance:

> $\frac{1}{6}$ of me is dancing,
> ballet, hip hop, and jazz.

Emily wrote about her attitude toward sports:

$\frac{1}{6}$ **of me is a player,**
who doesn't give up
and challenges myself
to do it, take the chance,
and shoot or score it.

Louise wrote about her strong friendships:

$\frac{1}{6}$ **of me is a friend.**
I'm a friend to a lot of friends
who compliment me on my friendship.

Some students wrote each verse from start to finish. Others wrote a phrase at the top of each verse—"$\frac{1}{6}$ of me is . . ."—and filled in the specific details later.

Some students said they weren't sure how to convert the facts into poetry. I told them not to think about that—just to write some details about each topic they chose. I encouraged them to choose details that would tell me something about them.

Here are three completely different poems that told me volumes about the students who wrote them:

Fractions of Me

$\frac{2}{6}$ **of me is an actress.**
I try out for a lot of plays
even though I don't like
some of the directors.

$\frac{2}{6}$ **of me is a singer.**
I sing in a choir and
in some plays and
sometimes I get solos.

$\frac{1}{6}$ **of me is a soccer player.**
Sometimes I get goals
and sometimes I don't.

$\frac{1}{6}$ **of me is a pack rat.**
It is hard for me
to get rid of things
and my room is a mess.

$\frac{2}{6} + \frac{2}{6} + \frac{1}{6} + \frac{1}{6} = \frac{6}{6}$
The whole of me.

Jennifer, grade 4

Fractions of Me

$\frac{2}{6}$ of me is athletic.
I play all day.
I play basketball in the fall.

$\frac{2}{6}$ of me is videogames.
I like to play basketball games
because it's my favorite sport.
I like the way they dribble
up and down the court.

$\frac{2}{6}$ of me is a big brother.
I'm the big brother because
we have no other brother.
I'm a twin.

All of the 6ths of me
$\frac{2}{6} + \frac{2}{6} + \frac{2}{6} =$ me,
the whole of me.

Khalid, grade 4

Fractions of Me

$\frac{3}{6}$ of me is a crowd cheering to me
like the high tide in an ocean.

$\frac{1}{6}$ of me is making an invention
like a robot talking.

$\frac{2}{6}$ of me is a smile
with a friend at a park
or anywhere else.

That's all of me.

$$\frac{3}{6} + \frac{1}{6} + \frac{2}{6} = \frac{6}{6}$$

Jason, grade 4

   I concluded that this is an excellent way to find out what makes students
tick, as well as a meaningful use of fractions.

Teacher Notes: Fractions of Me Poems

1. Explain to the students that they will be writing fraction poems called "Fractions of Me."

2. Display an overhead of the blank Poetry Frame picture, or recreate it on chart paper or on the board. Fill in the squares on the blank person to match those in my Sample Poem.

3. Draw in the face and hair. Put in the limbs and add a prop to show one of my interests, such as a pencil.

4. Pass out my Sample Poem and read it aloud. Make sure students notice that I give specific detail about the parts of me in order to make each verse interesting. Point out that I ended it by adding up all the fractions of me to make a whole.

5. Have the students create their own pictures and write their own poems telling about the fractions of themselves. It would be fun for them if you created a picture and poem about yourself as well.

6. Have volunteers share their poems with the class, or allow students to share informally with each other.

Easier and Harder

To make this easier, you can have 4 squares in the "Poetry Frame person" instead of 6. To make it harder, you can have 8 to 10 squares. You can also ask older students to reduce the fractions when writing the poem.

CHAPTER 11
Free-form Math Poems
POETRY FRAME

_____

_____

_____

_____

_____

_____

_____

_____

_____

_____

_____

_____

_____

_____

_____

Name _____

Classroom Journal: Free-form Math Poems

As an experiment, I let students write math poems about anything they wanted. I tried this out with a fourth-grade classroom and with small groups of individual students in other grades.

To start, I read the students a variety of math poems from my books *Counting Our Way to the 100th Day* (Margaret K. McElderry Books, 2004) and *Counting Caterpillars and Other Math Poems* (Scholastic, 1998). Next, we brainstormed topics in math that they could write about (see page 84). Some beautiful poetry resulted. The fourth-grade teacher, Janeen Swan, said that Adrien had never been so confident about his writing before. His poem sounds like a classical nursery rhyme:

> 60 dogs in the cities,
> 80 cats in the town and 15 kitties.
> all the cats chasing 20 rats,
> 30 frogs on some logs,
> How many dogs and frogs
> cats and rats are there
> altogether?
>
> *Adrien, grade 4*

Young Ju wrote a geometry poem:

The Puddle in the Gutter

> I like the puddle in the gutter
> because it's like a window
> but has no corners like a rectangle.
>
> I like the puddle in the gutter
> because when I plop a stone in,
> circles ripple in the puddle.
>
> I like the puddle in the gutter
> because I see the reflections of
> my oval face and
> the sphere white moon
> shining at night.
>
> I like the puddle in the gutter
> because the puddle likes this poem.
>
> *Young-Ju, grade 3*

Young Kuk wrote a poem that can be read as a multiplication or a division poem:

A Funny Squirrel Day

12 squirrels in trees
squawking over my head,
whispering secrets over my head,
wish I knew what.

12 squirrels in 3 trees,
smashing their nuts
with sharp teeth.

Four shells bonk me
on the head,
Four shells tumble down onto the lawn,
Four shells fly down onto the driveway.

Twelve squirrels pick up 12 nuts
for their shell collection.

Young Kuk, grade 5

Will wrote a fraction poem. Notice the pun in the last line.

Fraction Poem

"Moooooom! Anna ate half the pizza and now she's sick!"
And that's what I'm here to tell you about
(the fractions, not the pizza).

These tiny, little, itty-bitty things called fractions
are very popular these days.
Like in my life:
Fractions have taken over my bedtime
("Will, you are going to bed in half-an-hour.")
My violin time:
("Will, practice one-third of an hour.")
My cream pie:
("Moooooom, you ate one-fourth of the cream pie!")

First they've taken over my life.
Next they'll be taking over the *whole* world!

William, grade 4

Ji-Min was an ELL student. She has returned to her home in South Korea since writing this skillfully written, poignant poem in fourth grade.

How Many Birds?

Ten birds black birds on the wire
one two three four five
six seven eight nine ten birds

My brother young brother threw the rock
one rock

That rock one rock hit one bird small bird
one small bird

One bird small bird which got hit fell down
one small bird

How many birds black birds do you think
were left on the wire?
how many birds?

If you think there were nine birds left
you are wrong. There were none.

One bird hit and fell down
but other birds scared birds
flew away
far away.

Ji-Min, grade 4

I considered my experiment a success!

Teacher Notes: Free-form Math Poems

1. Read math poetry to the students. See the bibliography on page 136.
2. Brainstorm or list topics in math that they could write about.

addition	measurement
subtraction	money
multiplication	geometry
division	algebra
fractions	

3. Display a list of general content topics, shown below. This will help prime the pump.

nature	school
seasons	hobbies
animals	sports
science	food
friends	transportation
family	geography
feelings	colors

4. Have students write freely.
5. Invite volunteers to share.

Sadaf Rizvi

II
Teaching Mathematickles

Mathematickles are like math haiku. They are math problems with words instead of numbers. Writing mathematickles enables students to explore new frontiers of their imaginations and to deepen their understanding of math concepts. For some students, this will be the first time they understand or find mathematics appealing.

These unusual math haiku can be written by mainstream, ELL, and gifted students, on different levels. They will appeal to students with verbal, mathematical, and visual intelligence. They will make sense to abstract thinkers and students who perceive their world more concretely. Often, students are drawn to and understand mathematickles even better than adults. You may be surprised by student responses when they are given time to think about and write mathematickles.

To write mathematickles, follow these steps:

1. Choose an operation or a concept in mathematics.

2. Show samples of mathematickles. There are samples on the Poetry Frames and in the Classroom Journals. There are also samples in the children's picture book entitled *Mathematickles!* (Margaret K. McElderry Books, 2003).

3. List topics that would be rich with possibilities for writing mathematickles:

    ★ nature   ★ school
    ★ seasons   ★ hobbies
    ★ animals   ★ sports
    ★ science   ★ food
    ★ friends   ★ transportation
    ★ family   ★ geography
    ★ feelings   ★ colors

4. Write some mathematickles together.

5. Let students know that the words in mathematickles don't have to be nouns. They can be verbs, sounds, smells, tastes, textures, and more!

6. Distribute the Poetry Frames. Students can work individually or they can work in pairs or groups. I would especially recommend working together on multiplication and division mathematickles because they are the most challenging.

7. Circulate as students write. It works best if you remain very open-minded, accepting students' poems and mainly suggesting rearrangements of their words, rather than questioning the sense of their poems.

8. Have students revise and write final drafts.

9. Allow students time to share their results with each other. For fun, have students read only the problem, and let classmates guess the answer—like a riddle.

Example: zebra − stripes = _____

Yuka Sakazaki

C H A P T E R 12

Addition and Subtraction Mathematickles

Addition Poems

Addition poems put 2 or more things together.

> **broken pencil**
> **+   homework**
> **trouble**
>
> cat + mouse = scared mouse
> **3 green hearts + a green vine = a clover**
> frogs + night pond = summer concert
> **moon + stars =** _____

Angela, grade 2

Write an addition poem. Think about nature, animals, school, sports, friends, colors, or any topic you want.

_____ + _____ = _____

Write another addition poem. Some ideas include fruit salad, ice cream sundae, a family, a sandwich, and a book.

_____ + _____ = _____

More Fun
Write one that rhymes.
Here's an example:

> cries
> whines
> yowls
> **+ moans**
> **puppy dog left alone**

Name _____

Addition and Subtraction Mathematickles

Subtraction Poems

Subtraction poems take something away and show what is left.

$$\frac{\text{octopus} - \text{ink}}{\text{black cloud}} \qquad \frac{\text{Earth} - \text{animals}}{\text{sad Earth}}$$

baby − nap = crying

glimmering sea − sparkling water = soft, shiny sand

autumn trees − leaves = _____

David, grade 2

Write a subtraction poem. Think about seasons, nature, animals, school, sports, or any topic you want.

_____ + _____ = _____

Write another subtraction poem. Some ideas: The answer could be desert, snake, cold, yeah!, ouch! trouble, barking, hungry, bald, sad, happy, lonely, dark, or anything you think up.

_____ + _____ = _____

More Fun

Try addition and subtraction together:

seeds + water + sun − weeds = garden

_____ = _____

Name _____

Classroom Journal
Addition and Subtraction Mathematickles in the Mainstream and ELL Classroom

In a Mainstream Classroom

When I prepared a workshop for second grade, I wondered if writing mathematickles would work with young children. All the children's eyes were on me when I showed examples of addition and subtraction poems such as the ones below similar to those in my book *Mathematickles!* They had never seen anything like it but grasped the concept quickly.

housetops + fresh snowfall = white frosting

$$\frac{\text{birdhouse} - \text{birds}}{\text{seedsdroppingshusks}}$$

I passed out the Poetry Frames and we went over the examples. Then we discussed the metaphor in the poem about white frosting—how the snow on a roof can look like frosting. They thought of other images the snow looked like, such as soft clouds and white quilt. Then they explained the answer "stringfeatherstwigsleaves" to me, saying that a bird's nest is made of many materials all woven together.

On chart paper, we made a list of general topics and wrote some sample mathematickles as a group. Then everyone started writing, even ELL students. Here is a sampling from the second graders:

3 green hearts + a green vine = a clover   *Angela, grade 2*

Africa + BOOMBoom = drummaker somewhere   *Aaron, grade 2*

ice cream + sunny day = ice cream sunday   *Abigail, grade 2*

Earth – light = night   *Clifford, grade 2*

The teacher, Karen Lemoine, emphasizes rich language in her classroom, and at her urging, she and I encouraged children to add to their bare-bones poetry. For example, David first wrote "sea – water = sand." Then he changed it to the following poem:

glimmering sea – sparkling water = soft, shiny sand *David, grade 2*

Other children also added rich words to their mathematickles as well:

exquisite pattern on cloth + needle + thread = patterned pillow

Kavya, grade 2

sandcastles with pretty shells and oysters + giant foamy
waves = flat sands

Robin, grade 2

A few days later, I was mowing the lawn, when I came across a thriving bunch of sour grass with giant clover-like petals. They were perfect green hearts—something I would never have noticed before Angela's poem about clover.

In an ELL Classroom

A week later, Annette Isaacson, an ELL teacher, allowed me to observe while she introduced mathematickles to her second-grade students. She noted that. at the basic level, writing mathematickles poetry requires only a knowledge of nouns, and nouns are the easiest part of speech to use when learning a new language. She was very pleased with her students' poems:

2 long ears + pink nose + fluffy white tail = baby rabbit

Jasmine, grade 2

dog – bark = quiet please

Joshua, grade 2

worm + apple = crunch, crunch

Maria, grade 2

Annette said that Jasmine normally writes one-word answers and Joshua's work is usually difficult to understand. Joshua originally wrote just the word *quiet* as the answer of his poem. Then he asked me if he could make a joke and added the word *please*.

Annette also let me sit in while her ELL students in fifth grade wrote mathematickles. All but Jenny had been in the United States less than a year.

hill + roll = dizzy	*Jenny, grade 5*
eagle + red + white + green = flag	*Jenny, grade 5*
clouds + mountain = rain	*Claudia, grade 5*
cheese + tortilla = quesadilla	*Claudia, grade 5*
2 cats + 10 mice = 2 fat cats	*Ji-Min, grade 4*
night + fireworks = New Year's	*Ruize, grade 5*
zebra – stripes + little = foal	*Ruize, grade 5*

In the ELL room and in other classrooms, when I would try to intervene to help children, they would look at me as if to say, "I don't really need help. I'm thinking." I concluded that they were making connections in their minds about subjects they knew personally and felt strongly about. They needed time to formulate their thoughts. When they came up with an idea, I saw a twinkle in their eyes!

Teacher Notes
Addition Mathematickles

1. Talk about what addition does: Addition puts 2 or more things together.

2. Pass out the Poetry Frames.

3. Look over the sample poems. Think of other possible answers for

    housetops + fresh snowfall = _____

    For example, children might give answers such as *soft clouds* or
    white quilt.

4. Fill in the blank in this mathematickle:

    moon + stars = _____

    Possible answers are *nighttime, night sky, nightscape, skyscape, night lights.*

5. List topics that are good for writing addition mathematickles, such
    as nature, seasons, animals, friends, school, hobbies, sports, food,
    and colors.

6. Write an addition mathematickle together.

7. Have children write several mathematickles on the Poetry Frame.
    If they want to keep going, they can use the back of the paper.

8. For an extension, invite children to try writing mathematickles that
    rhyme.

Teacher Notes
Subtraction Mathematickles

1. Talk about what subtraction does: In subtraction you "take away" and see what's left.

2. Pass out the Poetry Frames.

3. Look over the Sample Poems. Think of other possible answers for

    Earth – animals = _____

    Some possibilities are *vegetarians*, *plants and people*, and *lonely people*.

4. Fill in the blank in this mathematickle together:

    autumn – leaves = _____

    Possible answers are *bare branches*, *sticks*, *bare arms*, *cold trees*, and so on.

5. List topics that are good for writing subtraction mathematickles, such as seasons, animals, friends, school, hobbies, sports, food, and colors.

6. Write a subtraction mathematickle together.

7. Have children write several mathematickles on the Poetry Frames. If they want to keep going, they can use the back of the paper.

8. For an extension, invite children to try using addition and subtraction together.

Tony Galicia

CHAPTER 13
Multiplication Mathematickles

Multiplication is more powerful than addition. It is repeated addition.

maggot
x time
_____
   fly   *Kevin, grade 5*

   hot
x rocks
_____
   lava   *Samantha, grade 5*

kernels x heat = popcorn

twigs x spark = _____

Now write a multiplication poem. Ideas: What makes a caterpillar into a butterfly, a tadpole into a frog, a hurricane, a forest fire, an earthquake?

_____ x _____ = _____

_____ x _____ = _____

_____ x _____ = _____

Name _____

Classroom Journal
Multiplication Mathematickles

In fourth- and fifth-grade workshops, I focused on writing multiplication mathematickles with the students. I started in the fifth grade, knowing that this would be challenging. First I showed the students samples and told them to stretch and loosen their minds.

shooting stars x darkness = nature's fireworks

woodpecker x rotten stump = birdworld rap

I explained that shooting stars and the reverberating sound of a woodpecker's rapping were *powerful* enough to be multiplication, rather than addition.

We brainstormed topics they could use for their own poetry, such as nature, seasons, science, food, sports, friends, school, and transportation. The students were so motivated, they began writing even before we'd finished generating ideas. Throughout the session, they shared spontaneously in confident voices, almost winking at me conspiratorially as if to say, "Wasn't that clever?" They wrote the whole time and most filled at least one page. I could hear the students' minds working as they composed.

Science provided rich material for their poems. In fact, science and mathematickles go very well together.

maggot
x   time
fly   *Kevin, grade 5*

hot
x rocks
lava   *Samantha, grade 5*

In a discussion of whether these poems were addition or multiplication, we all evolved in our understanding of the operations. We concurred with Kevin that the transformation of a maggot to a fly was definitely multiplication—it was too powerful to be addition. The same was true for the fiery process that created lava.

Subsequent to that workshop, I went into several fourth-grade classrooms, I not only read my own multiplication mathematickles, I also read the fifth-grade samples. With all these examples, the fourth graders came up with some powerful mathematickles that definitely sounded like math haiku.

I liked the poetic images in their mathematickles about nature. They engaged the senses so that you could see, feel, and smell their images:

fresh breeze x ocean = beach   *Jennifer, grade 4*

nature x treenap = treehouse   *Jason, grade 4*

nature x pinesmell = forest   *Jason, grade 4*

lightning x night = storm   *Ashvin, grade 4*

grass x dirt x rocks = mountain   *Ashvin, grade 4*

Other subject matter worked well, too:

books x garden = reading garden   *Ashvin, grade 4*

school x brain power = good education   *Emily, grade 4*

I agreed with Nan Knoblauch, one of the fourth-grade teachers, when she said that the students varied in the depth of their understanding of the form, but all of them seemed genuinely involved. Everyone shared voluntarily, even one girl who was cognitively impaired.

Nan commented, "Their personalities, their individualism, their interests come through and they *hear* each other. It's interesting to see who writes about *me* and who writes about the world at large."

When it was time for me to go, the students weren't ready to stop. In one class, the recess bell rang, and they were still at it: "Don't go, don't go," they said to me. "I have one more!" "Listen to this!"

Teacher Notes
Multiplication Mathematickles

1. Talk about what multiplication does. Multiplication is repeated addition.

2. Pass out the Poetry Frame.

3. Look over the Sample Poems.

4. Fill in the blank in the unfinished mathematickle:

    twigs x spark = _____

    Possible answers are *forest fire, campfire,* and *sad forest.*

5. List topics that are good for writing multiplication mathematickles: nature, science, seasons, animals, friends, and school.

6. Write a multiplication mathematickle together.

7. Have students write several mathematickles on the Poetry Frame. They can use the back of the page as well. Many will benefit from working in pairs or groups.

8. Encourage students to share their mathematickles.

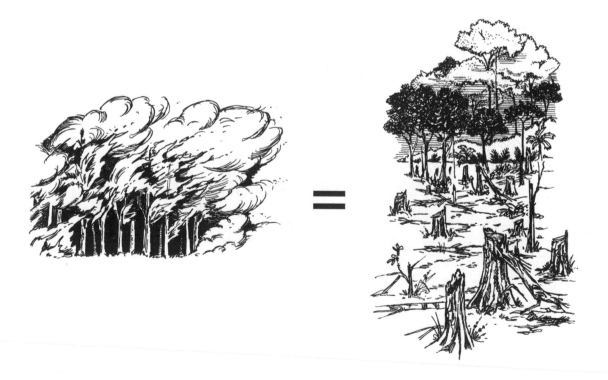

CHAPTER 14
Multiplication Tables Mathematickles

X	rain	snow
light	drizzle	snow flurry
heavy	downpour	blizzard

Try this table that has been started. You can change the words if you want to.

X	red	blue
hot		
cold		

Name _____

Multiplication Tables Mathematickles

This table has also been started. You can change the words if you want to.

X	cow	lion
female		
male		

Create a multiplication table of your own. Some ideas are weather, seasons, colors, temperatures, sizes, and weights.

Name _____

Classroom Journal
Multiplication Tables Mathematickles

I wasn't sure if fourth graders could do multiplication tables but they loved guessing the entries in the one I wrote below and the one in my picture book *Mathematickles!*, so I forged ahead:

X	rain	snow
light	drizzle	snow flurry
heavy	downpour	blizzard

The students came up with some interesting tables.

X	sink	float
ship	SOS	ok
fish	ok	dead

Brandon, grade 4

When I asked Brandon about his table above, he explained that someone near him was writing a mathematickle involving the SOS code so he started thinking about ships. He noticed that my times table had opposites (sun and rain) so he started thinking about the opposites *sinking* and *floating*. He thought to himself that a ship sinks and floats. He wondered, "What else sinks and floats? A fish!" I was so pleased to hear his thinking process. His observation about opposites would certainly help other students create tables of their own.

Jeremy came up with a thoughtful table about the differences in weather across the United States and the world.

X	winter	spring	summer	fall
2	Alaska	Florida	California	Massachusetts
3	Antarctica	Hawaii	Africa	Vermont

Jeremy, grade 4

To help students with their writing, I thought up a few "starters" on the Poetry Frames.

Teacher Notes
Multiplication Tables Mathematickles

1. Pass out the Poetry Frames.

2. Let students explain the sample multiplication table.

3. Read through the "starter tables." Make sure the students understand they can change or add to the animals and colors. Here is a good Web site for names of males, females, and baby animals:

> http://www.enchantedlearning.com/subjects/animals/
> Animalbabies.shtml

Below are some possibilities:

> horse: stallion, mare, colt or filly
> pig: boar, sow, piglet
> seal: bull, sow, pup
> whale: bull, cow, calf
> sheep: buck or ram, ewe, lamb
> goose: gander, goose, gosling
> deer: buck, doe, fawn
> lion: lion, lioness, cub

4. Point out the blank table on the Poetry Frame. Suggest a few possible topics, such as weather, seasons, color, temperature, sizes, and weights. Read Brandon's description of his thinking process on page 99 to start students thinking about opposites in their tables.

CHAPTER 15
Simple Division and Inverse Operations Mathematickles

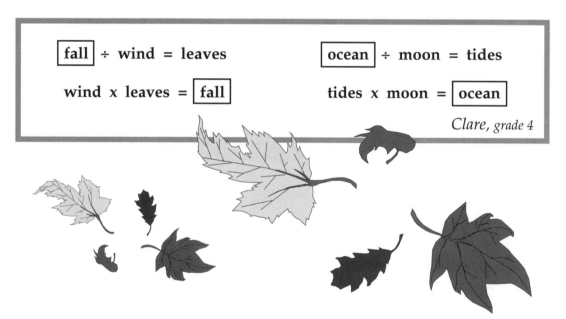

fall ÷ wind = leaves   ocean ÷ moon = tides

wind x leaves = fall   tides x moon = ocean

Clare, grade 4

Write multiplication and division mathematickles that are inverses of each other.

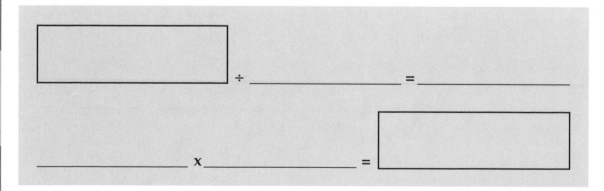

÷ _____ = _____

_____ x _____ =

Name _____

Simple Division and Inverse Operations Mathematickles

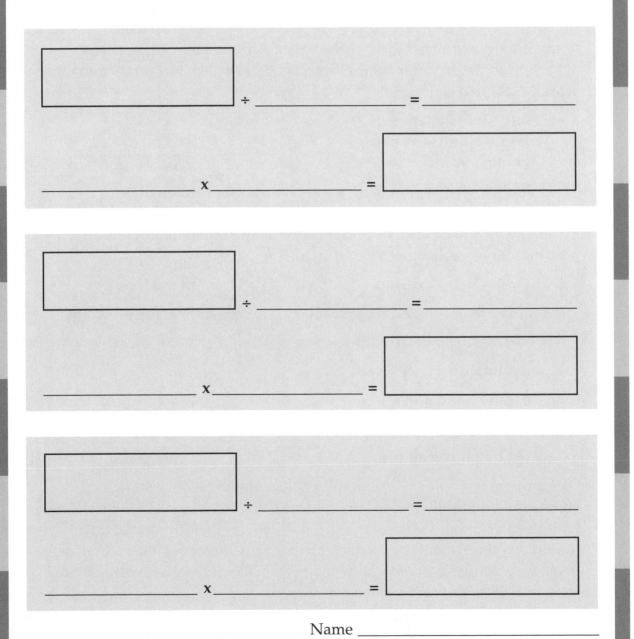

Name _____

Classroom Journal
Simple Division and Inverse Operations Mathematickles

In the fourth grade I started with some simple division mathematickles because I knew division mathematickles were the most challenging of all. First I used the radical sign ($\overline{)\quad}$) but that was too advanced. Many of the students didn't know how to read it. They tended to read it as the divisor divided by the dividend, instead of the other way around. We ended up using the ÷ sign because they could read their mathematickles poems much more easily.

I showed the students some examples I had written and some from other workshops I had conducted:

fall ÷ wind = leaves
lake ÷ storm = ripples
books ÷ words = stories   *Jordan, grade 4*

I told them they would need to loosen their minds to do division mathematickles, and they all agreed to give it a try. The students were genuinely intrigued, and the activity sparked their imaginations. Morgan, who likes to be challenged, started writing immediately.

glass ÷ sea = sea glass   *Morgan, grade 4*

Some students worked very creatively with geographic features:

water ÷ rock = waterfall   *Jason, grade 4*

mountain ÷ crater = valley   *Clare, grade 4*

ocean ÷ sand = beach   *Lauren, grade 4*

Emily took off in a different direction:

road ÷ car = road trip   *Emily, grade 4*

I thought it would be beneficial to follow up the next week with a workshop specifically focused on division being the reverse of multiplication. I felt that they would understand division better if they combined it with multiplication. When I was making up examples, I realized the concept of inverse operations worked best in mathematickles if the dividend was a big concept like *fall* or the *sky* or the *ocean*.

$\boxed{\text{fall}}$ ÷ wind = leaves

wind x leaves = $\boxed{\text{fall}}$

When I returned to the class, I talked about the dividend using numbers first. I explained to them that in $15 \div 3 = 5$, the biggest number comes first. The biggest number, the dividend, is the one that is divided. They showed me how to reverse it and make the division fact into a multiplication fact: $3 \times 5 = 15$.

I put a box around the 15 to mimic the worksheet:

$$\boxed{15} \div 3 = 5$$

$$3 \times 5 = \boxed{15}$$

I told the students that if we wanted to make mathematickles with words instead of numbers, we needed to put the big-concept words in the boxes. We tested it out:

$$\boxed{\text{winter}} \div \text{clouds} = \text{snow flurries}$$

$$\text{clouds} \times \text{snow flurries} = \boxed{\text{winter}}$$

$$\boxed{\text{garden}} \div \text{rows} = \text{veggies}$$

$$\text{rows} \times \text{veggies} = \boxed{\text{garden}}$$

$$\boxed{\text{flowers}} \div \text{bees} = \text{pollen}$$

$$\text{bees} \times \text{pollen} = \boxed{\text{flowers}}$$

We brainstormed big topics and came up with words like *winter, spring, summer, fall, ocean, mountains, forest, storm, time,* and *school*. I passed out the Poetry Frames and most students ended up filling up one or two frames. They were motivated!

When they showed me their poems, I challenged some of the students to rearrange their initial poem, making sure that the largest concept was written in the box on the Poetry Frame. I encouraged them to experiment with the three words they were using for their poem, trying the words in different positions.

Erik's and Clare's were quite profound:

future ÷ time = past
past x time = future *Erik, grade 4*

bird ÷ time = bird egg
bird egg x time = bird *Erik, grade 4*

night ÷ time = day
day x time = night *Erik and Clare, grade 4*
(These students worked independently.)

ocean ÷ moon = tides
tides x moon = ocean *Clare, grade 4*

Some remainders naturally popped up in the division mathematickles and we rewrote them under the radical sign. Zandra originally had "people getting wet" as her remainder, but I challenged her to come up with one word, and she rose to the challenge.

$$\text{wind } \overline{)\,\text{storm}} \quad \text{rain R puddles}$$

Zandra, grade 4

$$\text{moon } \overline{)\,\text{ocean}} \quad \text{tides R beach}$$

Clare, grade 4

$$\text{pencil } \overline{)\,\text{story}} \quad \text{writer R spelling problems}$$

Kelly, grade 4

$$\text{wind } \overline{)\,\text{trees}} \quad \text{baretrees R leaves all over}$$

Clare, grade 4

By the time we were done, we all understood the inverse operations of multiplication and division, and the meaning of remainders, much better than we had before.

Annie Ouyang

Teacher Notes
Simple Division and Inverse Operations Mathematickles

1. Talk about what division does. Division divides something into equal parts.

2. Show numerical examples of multiplication and division as inverse operations:

$$15 \div 3 = 5 \qquad\qquad 3 \times 5 = 15$$

   Emphasize that 15, the largest number, is the one being divided. It is the dividend.

3. Brainstorm "big concept words" (or big topics) that could be the dividend in division mathematickles. Here are some possibilities:

winter	orchard
spring	cave
summer	storm
sky	time
ocean	night
beach	day
mountains	library
lake	playground
pond	school
forest	books
woods	United States
rainforest	

4. Pass out the Poetry Frame. Go over the examples of inverse operations on the Poetry Frame. Make sure students realize that the "biggest-concept word" goes in the box.

5. Work together to write a mathematickle showing inverse operations and/or show your favorite examples from the Classroom Journal.

6. Have students write their own inverse operation mathematickles on the Poetry Frame. They can write extras on the back. Many will benefit from working in pairs or groups.

CHAPTER 16
Long Division Mathematickles

Division is the action of separating something into equal parts. Sometimes there is a remainder.

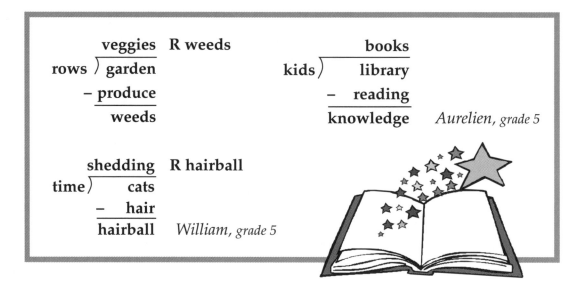

$$\text{rows} \overline{)\begin{array}{c} \text{veggies} \quad \text{R weeds} \\ \text{garden} \\ -\ \text{produce} \\ \hline \text{weeds} \end{array}}$$

$$\text{kids} \overline{)\begin{array}{c} \text{books} \\ \text{library} \\ -\ \text{reading} \\ \hline \text{knowledge} \end{array}}$$

Aurelien, grade 5

$$\text{time} \overline{)\begin{array}{c} \text{shedding} \quad \text{R hairball} \\ \text{cats} \\ -\ \text{hair} \\ \hline \text{hairball} \end{array}}$$

William, grade 5

Write long division mathematickles of your own.

1. ▶

2. ▶

Name _____

Classroom Journal
Long Division Mathematickles

Encouraged by my success with division mathematickles in grade four, I developed a lesson about long division with remainders for a fifth-grade classroom. Gaelyn Mason, the teacher, was as delighted and open-minded as the students. She just warned them not to use crude language. I ended up giving workshops in her class during two different years.

The first year, I showed examples similar to the ones in my book *Mathematickles!*:

$$\text{rows} \overline{)\;\text{garden}} \quad \begin{array}{l} \text{veggies} \quad \text{R weeds} \\ \hline \end{array}$$

$$\begin{array}{r} \textbf{veggies} \quad \textbf{R weeds} \\ \textbf{rows} \,\overline{)\,\textbf{garden}} \\ -\,\underline{\textbf{produce}} \\ \textbf{weeds} \end{array}$$

The fifth graders came up with terrific mathematickles:

$$\begin{array}{r} \textbf{pop!} \quad \textbf{R air} \\ \textbf{hole} \,\overline{)\,\textbf{balloon}} \end{array}$$

Rachael, grade 5

$$\begin{array}{r} \textbf{books} \\ \textbf{kids} \,\overline{)\,\textbf{library}} \\ -\,\underline{\textbf{reading}} \\ \textbf{knowledge} \end{array}$$

Aurelien, grade 5

The concept of a remainder in division became much clearer to everyone when we analyzed and admired the remainders in the poems written by Rachel and Aurelien above. We studied all the different stages of Aurelien's because he had shown all the steps of a long division problem. We agreed that for long division in mathematickles you needed to loosen your mind a little and add some imagination to the mix.

The next year, I went into Ms. Mason's fifth-grade class again and used examples from her former fifth graders, along with examples from *Mathematickles!* The class had been studying long division for several weeks. In the middle of the class, I reinforced the process of solving or writing a division problem by showing an example on the board (at right).

$$\begin{array}{r} 3 \\ 4 \,\overline{)\,13} \\ -\,\underline{12} \\ 1 \end{array}$$

I pointed out that 13 is the largest number. I talked about how you get the 12 by multiplying 3 x 4. I wanted them to see that they would be doing something similar in their long division mathematickles. We also reviewed how to read a division problem by starting with the dividend.

Sometimes, a student would come up with a group of interesting words and would rearrange them in different ways to make them work as a long division problem. Ashley, who had trouble with mathematickles at first, really went to town in this session. She worked with the following words: *universe, planets, space, 9 planets,* and *stars.* She knew the remainder was stars. Here's what she ended up with:

```
                space   R stars
      planets ) universe
           − 9 planets
              stars
```

Ashley, grade 5

Others students dove into the writing as well. The dividend and the divisor were easiest and often they had a clever remainder in mind. But filling out the whole problem took a lot of thought.

Students chose topics that were of particular interest to them. William, a cat owner, often writes about cats:

```
         shedding   R hairball
    time )    cats
         −    hair
         hairball
```

William, grade 5

It thundered outside during the workshop, and Alex wrote this one:

```
              boom   R rain
    lightning ) clouds
            − sparks
              rain
```

Alex, grade 5

Conor was very involved in his subject matter:

```
           mutant   R aliens
    future )  people
          − predator
           aliens
```

Conor, grade 5

If you relax your mind, you'll see the sheer beauty in Paige's:

```
          lake   R bay
    pond ) ocean
         − gulf
           bay
```

Paige, grade 5

I could almost hear the gears in the students' minds turning as they wrote their intriguing long division mathematickles.

Teacher Notes
Long Division Mathematickles

1. Talk about long division. Show a problem using numbers such as the one below:

$$4 \,\overline{)\, 13} \quad \begin{array}{r} 3 \\ \hline -\, 12 \\ \hline 1 \end{array}$$

Be sure to discuss the fact that in the problem, the 12 comes from 3 x 4; in other words, the quotient times the divisor equals 12. This will help them simulate this in their mathematickles (although it's a challenge. In the example, below, books x kids = reading:

$$\text{kids} \,\overline{)\, \text{library}} \quad \begin{array}{r} \text{books} \\ \hline -\ \text{reading} \\ \hline \text{knowledge} \end{array}$$

2. Pass out the Poetry Frame and go over the samples together.

3. List topics that are good for writing long division mathematickles: nature, science, seasons, animals, geography, colors, outer space, and school.

4. Write a long division mathematickle together if that will help.

5. Tell students that these will take a lot of thought. Even when they come up with one, they might have to juggle around some of the words, putting them in different positions until they work.

6. Have students show their mathematickles to a partner.

CHAPTER 17
Fractions and Geometry Mathematickles

$\frac{1}{3}$ moth = larva

$\frac{1}{3}$ ant = thorax

Kevin, grade 5

cone + $\frac{1}{2}$ sphere = ice cream cone

Soumya, grade 4

ocean + $\frac{1}{2}$ circle of rocks = a cove

Kelly, grade 4

Write your own fraction mathematickles.

Write your own geometry mathematickles.

They might be in the same poem.

_____

_____

_____

Name _____

Classroom Journal
Fractions and Geometry Mathematickles

I first introduced fractions and geometry mathematickles in a fifth-grade class, but because it was in the context of many types of mathematickles, most students opted to write mathematickles related to the operations. However, I remember one boy, Kevin, who was interested in science. He read his to the class, "$\frac{1}{3}$ ant = thorax," and we were all amazed.

For my next workshop, I visited a fourth-grade class. This time I read them only mathematickles I had written related to fractions and geometry. I told them it would be challenging to write their own and emphasized that it was good to take a risk. They rose to the challenge. Everyone gave it their best shot.

I explained that they could write fraction mathematickles and geometry mathematickles separately, or they could combine them.

Then I used the overhead to show some fraction samples. I included Kevin's.

$\frac{1}{3}$ moth = larva

$\frac{1}{2}$ day = morning

$\frac{1}{3}$ ant = thorax

Kevin, grade 5

Next we had a discussion about geometry because I thought it might be fun to write fraction and geometry mathematickles together, rather than separately. Some students didn't know the term *geometry*. One of the students explained that it was about shapes, and I added the topics of symmetry and angles. We listed two- and three-dimensional shapes on the board: circle, triangle, square, rectangle, pentagon, hexagon, sphere, cube, rectangular prism, cylinder, cone, and pyramid. Then I showed them some samples of geometry mathematickles:

$$\begin{array}{r} \textbf{hexagons} \\ \underline{\times\quad \textbf{buzzing}} \\ \textbf{thriving hive} \end{array}$$

squares x 4 + diamond = baseball field

After I posted the list of general topics for mathematickles, such as nature, science, school, sports, and transportation, the students immediately picked up on the topic of sports. When I looked around the room, I could see that many of the students were outstanding athletes, girls and boys. Some even included each other's names in their poems, after getting permission.

hexagons + sphere = soccerball	*Maile, grade 4*
sphere + net = goal	*Jennifer, grade 4*
Maile + sphere = goal	*Khalid, grade 4*
Jason + sphere = homerun	*Maile, grade 4*

Louise explained the triangle was the seat of the unicycle in her mathematickle:

circle + triangle = unicycle	*Louise, grade 4*

Themes other than sports evolved as well. The students were deep in thought. I tried to help a student with an empty page, and he said he was thinking. By the end of the period, he had figured out that a camera broke down into a rectangular solid and a cylinder.

Some students wrote geometry mathematickles:

1 trillion rays + circle = sun	*Louise, grade 4*
cylinders x 10 = a plate of pasta	*Zandra, grade 4*
circle + petals = flower	*Emma, grade 4*
2 rectangles x 1 = a book	*Clare, grade 4*
square + triangle = little house	*Kelly, grade 4*
happy face – face + cone = ice cream cone	*Andrew, grade 4*

Some combined fractions and geometry:

$\frac{1}{2}$ **sphere + cone = ice cream cone**	*Soumya, grade 4*
cylinder + $\frac{1}{2}$ bread = hot dog	*Louise, grade 4*

Kelly's was a particularly beautiful image:

ocean + $\frac{1}{2}$ circle of rocks = a cove	*Kelly, grade 4*

There was much interaction between students. They wanted to show each other their work and explain it to me as well.

Oleg wrote a geometry mathematickle from an operations point of view. He had generated many many ideas. But when he created the origami mathematickle, he knew he had come up with something particularly meaningful:

paper x fold + origami = shell	*Oleg, grade 4*

I decided it was worthwhile to introduce fractions and geometry mathematickles in a workshop of their own.

Teacher Notes
Fractions and Geometry Mathematickles

1. Explain to students that they will be writing fraction and geometry mathematickles. Help them understand what geometry is at their level (perhaps shapes and symmetry and possibly angles).

2. Pass out the Poetry Frame and go over the examples together. Explain that students can do fractions and geometry separately or together.

3. List topics that are good for writing fraction and/or geometry mathematickles: nature, science, seasons, animals, sports, food, space, and transportation.

4. Let students write their own mathematickles on the Poetry Frame. Share some of the ideas to spark the imaginations of everyone in the room.

5. Invite students to share their creations with someone sitting near them.

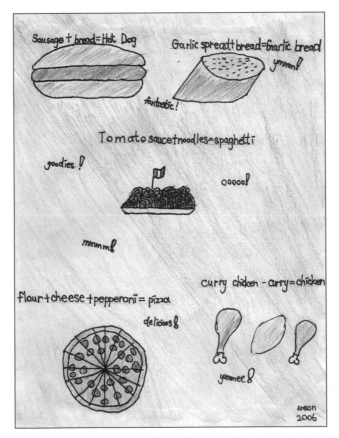

Anson Cheung

CHAPTER 18
Graphing Mathematickles

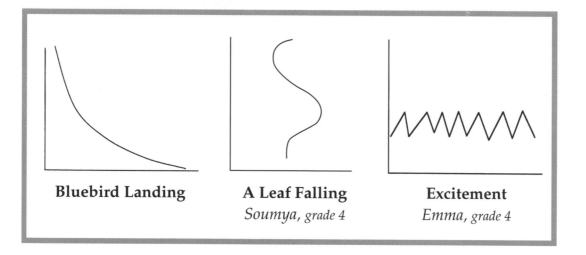

Bluebird Landing

A Leaf Falling
Soumya, grade 4

Excitement
Emma, grade 4

Create your own graphing mathematickles.

Name _____

Classroom Journal
Graphing Mathematickles

It was very exciting to write graphing mathematickles with a fourth-grade class. The students were very visual!

First, I showed an example from *Mathematickles*!

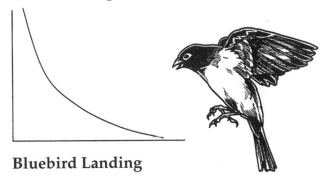

Bluebird Landing

One girl, Emma, was quietly doing amazing work. I had never thought of graphing emotions until she showed me her graph of "Excitement."

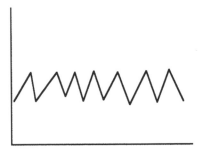

Excitement   *Emma, grade 4*

After I displayed her graph on the overhead, others followed suit with very creative graphs.

All of these graphs are a great precursor to algebra. They show that graphs can have different shapes.

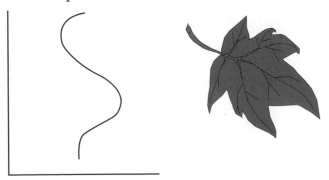

A Leaf Falling   *Soumya, grade 4*

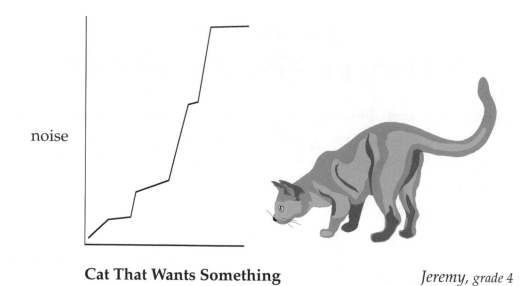

noise

Cat That Wants Something

Jeremy, grade 4

I loved Justin's, which told a story that he could totally relate to.

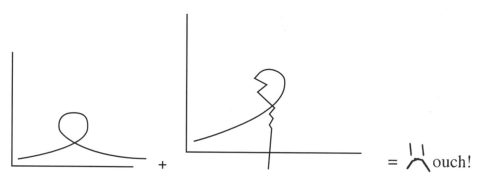

good skateboard trick mess-up

Justin, grade 4

= ouch!

Teacher Notes
Graphing Mathematickles

1. Explain to students that they will be writing graphing mathematickles.

2. Pass out the Poetry Frame and go over the examples together. Explain that they can work on another piece of paper if their graphs take up more room than is available on the Poetry Frame.

3. Have them note the titles of the sample graphs.

4. List topics that are good for writing graphing mathematickles: nature, seasons, animals, hobbies, transportation, emotions, or any topic that interests them. They can even tell a story.

5. Let students create their own graphs on the Poetry Frame. Share some of their ideas with the class to generate energy in the room.

6. Have students show their creations to someone sitting near them. Or have everyone leave their work on their desks. Then the students can circulate around and admire each other's work.

CHAPTER 19
Algebra Mathematickles: The Properties

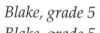

Commutative Property

$$a + b = b + a$$

sun + lotion = lotion + sun   *Blake, grade 5*
cookies + milk = milk + cookies   *Blake, grade 5*
dance + sing = sing + dance   *Paige, grade 5*

_____ + _____ = _____ + _____

_____ + _____ = _____ + _____

Associative Property

$$a + (b + c) = (a + b) + c$$

(jeans + shirt) + shoes = jeans + (shirt + shoes) = stylish

Alyssa, grade 5

(marshmallow + chocolate) + graham cracker = marshmallow + (chocolate + graham cracker)

Carly, grade 5

(_____ + _____) + _____ = _____ + (_____ + _____)

Name _____

Algebra Mathematickles: The Properties

Distributive Property

$$a \times (b + c) = a \times b + a \times c$$

light x (day + night) = sun + moon
books x (crime + princesses) = mystery + fantasy   *Sarah, grade 5*
fun x (mountains + ocean) = _____ + _____

_____ x (_____ + _____) = _____ + _____

Zero Property

$$n + 0 = n$$

green + clear = green   *Ashley, grade 5*
box + empty = box   *Alex, grade 5*

_____ + _____ = _____

Identity Property

$$n \times 1 = n$$

lake x drop of water = lake
school x work = school   *Kyle, grade 5*
sea of cats x cat = sea of cats   *William, grade 5*

_____ x _____ = _____

Name _____

Algebra Mathematickles: The Properties

Additive Inverse

$$n + (-n) = 0$$

walking forward + walking back = same spot   *Alex, grade 5*
doing homework + losing it = 0 credit   *Alyssa, grade 5*
built + destroyed = 0   *Thomas, grade 5*

_____ + _____ = _____

Transitive Property of Equality

If $a = b$ and $b = c$ then $a = c$

If cat = meow
and meow = hungry
then cat = hungry

If snake = reptile
and reptile = cold-blooded
then snake = cold-blooded   *Alyssa, grade 5*

If _____

and _____

then _____

Name _____

Classroom Journal
Algebra Mathematickles: The Properties

Ryan Peterson is an innovative math teacher in a middle school near my home. He developed an assignment for his eighth-grade algebra students using my book *Mathematickles!* His students wrote mathematickles based on the algebraic properties, with amazing results.

When I went to the fifth graders to introduce algebra mathematickles, I used the eighth-grade results as samples, along with some samples of my own. I devised a worksheet and began my experiment. I introduced some properties the students had already studied and some they hadn't. We carefully went over the examples on the Poetry Frame, which now includes some of the fifth graders' work.

I posted a list of general topics that they could choose from, such as food, nature, animals, sports, and hobbies. I asked them what their hobbies were to help them get started on the Poetry Frame.

In general, we agreed that the commutative property was fairly easy. They came up with mathematickles that had meaning to them:

$a + b = b + a$

cookies + milk = milk + cookies *Blake, grade 5*

ice + skates = skates + ice = ice skater *Sarah, grade 5*

One of the challenging properties was the associative property, but Priscilla's and Alyssa's worked very well. Priscilla's emphasized the power of teamwork:

$(a + b) + c = a + (b + c)$

(team + kick) + soccer ball = team + (kick + soccer ball) = goal

Priscilla, grade 5

(jeans + shirt) + shoes = shoes + (shirt + jeans) = stylish

Alyssa, grade 5

Interestingly enough, the distributive property seems clearer in words than in numbers or letters.

$a \times (b + c) = a \times b + a \times c$

We filled in the blank on the Poetry Frame together. They came up with the words *hiking* and *swimming* for the answer.

$a \times (b + c) = a \times b + a \times c$

fun x (mountains + ocean) = _____ + _____

Once we had completed the sample together, they went on to create some great poems. Blake is an aspiring artist, so of course his was about doodling, his favorite pastime.

books x (crime + princesses) = mystery + fantasy   *Sarah, grade 5*

fun x (me + pencil) = happy + doodle   *Blake, grade 5*

When I asked Ashley how she was doing on the Poetry Frame, she said her mind didn't work this way (in the way it took to write mathematickles) but she eventually came up with a good example for the Zero Property. She was very pleased that her mind had clicked in to the process.

$n + 0 = n$

green + clear = green   *Ashley, grade 5*

box + empty = box   *Alex, grade 5*

The students came up with interesting examples for the Identity Property:

$n \times 1 = n$

school x work = school   *Kyle, grade 5*

sea of cats x cat = sea of cats   *William, grade 5*

The Additive Inverse was new for them but they could certainly relate to it.

$n + (-n) = 0$

learning + forgetting = 0   *Sarah, grade 5*

built + destroyed = 0   *Thomas, grade 5*

walking forward + walking back = same spot   *Alex, grade 5*

The students had never seen the Transitive Property of Equality either. Alyssa's was particularly clear:

If $a = b$
and $b = c$
then $a = c$

If cat = meow
and meow = hungry
then cat = hungry   *Alyssa, grade 5*

The teacher, Gaelyn Mason, said, "Their minds are still open. They're not intimidated by creativity. They go for 'whatever' answer, it doesn't have to be the 'right' answer." She created a very open environment in her classroom that fostered creativity, and it showed in her students' work.

The students didn't want to turn in their papers. They continued to write on the backs of the sheets. Emily said, "That was fun!"

It surely was. Their poems were so good, I changed the worksheet to include their mathematickles.

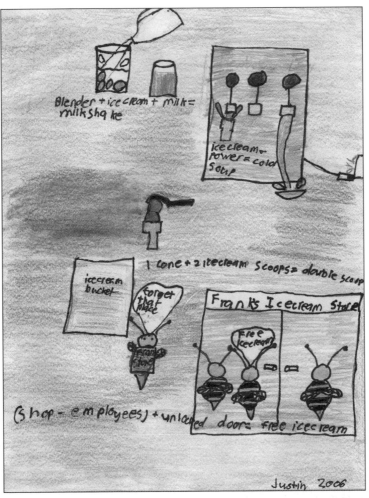

Justin Ziebell

Teacher Notes
Algebra Mathematickles: The Properties

1. Talk about the algebraic properties.

2. Pass out and use the Poetry Frame to show how the properties can be made into mathematickles.

3. Go over the examples together. Because the distributive property is one of the most challenging, initially, do the unfinished example together. Writing mathematickles can actually make the distributive property more understandable in the long run.

4. List topics that are good for writing algebra mathematickles: nature, science, seasons, animals, sports, hobbies, and food.

5. Give the students time to create algebra mathematickles on the Poetry Frame. They can complete them in any order they choose.

6. Have students show their results to a partner and/or read their poems out loud to the class.

CHAPTER 20

Algebra Mathematickles: The Unknown

Step 1:
mountain + cloud = rain

Claudia, grade 5

Step 2:
If mountain + n = rain
then n = cloud

Step 1:

_____ + _____ = _____

Step 2:
If _____

then n = _____

Step 1:
Earth – animals = sad planet

Step 2:
If Earth – n = sad planet,
then n = animals

Step 1:

_____ – _____ = _____

Step 2:
If _____

then n = _____

Name _____

Algebra Mathematickles: The Unknown

Step 1:
hot x rocks = lava   *Samantha, grade 5*

Step 2:
If hot x n = lava,
then n = rocks

Step 1:

_____ x _____ = _____

Step 2:
If _____

then n = _____

Step 1:
autumn ÷ wind = leaves

Step 2:
If autumn ÷ n = leaves,
then n = _____

Step 1:

_____ ÷ _____ = _____

Step 2:
If _____

then n = _____

Name _____

Classroom Journal
Algebra Mathematickles: The Unknown

In Gaelyn Mason's fifth grade, we worked again with algebra mathematickles, this time with the unknown, which we called n. I showed them examples of addition, subtraction, multiplication, and division mathematickles as a review.

mountain + cloud = rain *Claudia, grade 5*

Earth – animals = sad planet

hot x rocks = lava *Samantha, grade 5*

autumn ÷ wind = leaves

Then we transformed the equations to algebraic sentences by inserting an unknown. Step 1 was to write a mathematickle.

Step 1:
mountain + cloud = rain *Claudia, grade 5*

Step 2 was to transform it into an algebraic equations with a variable, or unknown.

Step 2:
If mountain + n = rain,
then n = cloud

(Note that n can represent any word in the equation.)

Addition

The students' poems reflected their personalities:

Carly's was funny:

> **cookie jar + kid = sugar rush**
> **If n + kid = sugar rush, then n = cookie jar**
>   *Carly, grade 5*

Blake finds homework stressful:

> **child + homework = stress**
> **If child + n = stress, then n = homework**
>   *Blake, grade 5*

Thomas is into science:

> **horse + donkey = mule**
> **If horse + n = mule, then n = donkey**
>   *Thomas, grade 5*

Jenny Isupov

Subtraction

forest – trees = plains
If forest – *n* = plains, then *n* = trees   *Sarah, grade 5*

cats – intelligence = dogs
If cats – *n* = dogs, then *n* = intelligence   *William, grade 5*

Asaf likes to talk. He wrote a mathematickle that had emotion in it:

Asaf – mouth = sadness
If *n* – mouth = sadness then *n* = Asaf   *Asaf, grade 5*

Kyle – videogames = bored Kyle
If Kyle – *n* = bored Kyle, then *n* = videogames   *Kyle, grade 5*

Earth – sun = new ice age
If *n* – sun = new ice age, then *n* = Earth   *Thomas, grade 5*

Anthony Barrera

Multiplication

Blake, the excellent artist, wrote about his favorite activity, drawing and doodling:

> **me** x **pencil** = **doodle fiend**
> **If me** x n = **doodle fiend, then** n = **pencil**   *Blake, grade 5*

> **snowman** x **sun** = **big puddle**
> **If snowman** x n = **big puddle, then** n = **sun**   *Ashley, grade 5*

> **seeds** x **water** = **plants**
> **If seeds** x n = **plants, then** n = **water**   *Sarah, grade 5*

Florida was experiencing hurricanes at the time of this workshop. So Alex brought in current events:

> **Florida** x **hurricane** = **windy**
> **If Florida** x n = **windy then** n = **hurricane**   *Alex, grade 5*

> **school** x **kids** = **knowledge**
> **If** n x **kids** = **knowledge, then** n = **school**   *Kyle, grade 5*

Christian Huard

Division

I ended up showing them a few division examples to help them with the division portion of the Poetry Frame:

balloon ÷ hole = pop!   *Rachael (excerpt), grade 5*

books ÷ words = stories   *Jordan, grade 4*

water ÷ rock = waterfall   *Jason, grade 4*

autumn ÷ wind = leaves

Here are some of their results. They did a great job.

purple ÷ red = blue
If purple ÷ *n* = blue then *n* = red   *Paige, grade 5*

Will told me that there's a theory that chickens evolved from T. Rex. He wrote his based on this theory:

chicken ÷ time = T. Rex
If chicken ÷ *n* = T. Rex then *n* = time   *William, grade 5*

snow ÷ skiers = trails
If *n* ÷ skiers = trails, then *n* = snow   *Kyle, grade 5*

This proved to be an excellent review of operations and algebra concepts for a group of creative, energetic fifth graders.

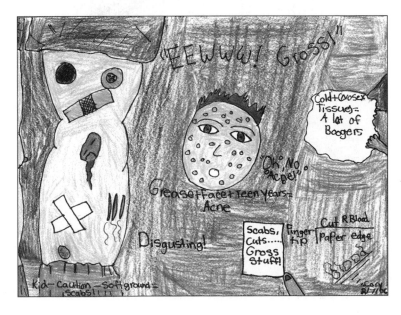

Cory Gaytan

Teacher Notes
Algebra Mathematickles:
The Unknown

1. Talk about the unknown in algebra.

2. Pass out the Poetry Frame.

3. Show the students addition, subtraction, multiplication, and division mathematickles as a review. Then explain that they will be writing mathematickles and substituting the unknown (*n*) for one of the words in their poems.

4. Go over the Poetry Frame with them.

5. Give them lots of examples of division mathematickles (see page 70 of the Classroom Journal) because this is the most challenging part.

6. List topics that are good for writing algebra mathematickles about the unknown: school, friends, sports, hobbies, colors, and food.

7. Have students fill in their Poetry Frames. They can complete the poems in any order.

Elana Loeb

Conclusion

Writing math poetry will wake up everyone in the classroom and change children's attitudes. The way all children dive into the Poetry Frames will surprise you, as will the depth of understanding that results. You'll find that everyone can shine because they will be writing from a place that they understand, whether it be a verbal or a logical place. The poets in the room will find that math is fun. The mathematicians will discover that writing poetry is fun.

Mainstream, ELL, and verbally challenged students will write beautiful poems that they can be proud of. Your time will definitely be well spent!

Minji Choi

Bibliography

Dodds, Dayle Ann. *The Great Divide, A Mathematical Marathon*. Cambridge: Candlewick Press, 2005.

Dodds, Dayle Ann. *The Shape of Things*. Cambridge: Candlewick Press, 1994.

Franco, Betsy. *Counting Caterpillars and Other Math Poems*. New York: Scholastic, 1999.

Franco, Betsy. *Counting Our Way to the Hundredth Day!* New York: Margaret K. McElderry Books, 2004.

Franco, Betsy. *Mathematickles!* New York: Margaret K. McElderry Books, 2003.

Franco, Betsy. *100 Seagulls Make a Racket*. Chicago: ETA/Cuisenaire, 2003.

Franco, Betsy. *Shadow Shapes*. Chicago: ETA/Cuisenaire, 2003.

Franco, Betsy. *Twins*. Chicago: ETA/Cuisenaire, 2003.

Hopkins, Lee Bennett, selected by. *Marvelous Math*. New York: Simon & Schuster, 1997.

Hulme, Joy N. *Counting by Kangaroos: A Multiplication Concept Book*. New York: W. H. Freeman & Co., 1995.

Hulme, Joy N. *Wild Fibonacci: Nature's Secret Code Revealed!* Berkeley: Tricycle Press, 2005.

Hulme, Joy N. *Sea Squares*. New York: Hyperion Press, 1993.

Hulme, Joy N. *Sea Sums*. New York: Disney Press, 1996.

Liatsos, Sandra. *Poems to Count On*. New York: Scholastic, 1999.

Murphy, Stuart J. *Divide and Ride (Mathstart 3)*. New York: HarperTrophy, 1997.

Tang, Greg. *The Best of Times*. New York: Scholastic, 2002.

Tang, Greg. *Math Fables*. New York: Scholastic, 2004.

Tang, Greg. *Math for All Seasons*. New York: Scholastic, 2003.

Tang, Greg. *Math-Terpieces*. New York: Scholastic, 2003.